AN EARLIER LIFE

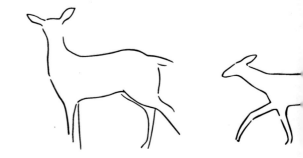

Praise for Brenda Miller

"Delicate, elegant, and occasionally devastating, Brenda Miller's essays are helping to set the standard for our generation."

—*John D'Agata*

"A master essayist at the top of her game."

—*Harrison Candelaria Fletcher*

"Brenda Miller writes with such extraordinary grace and intimacy that, despite our weariness and fears, we find ourselves falling in love with the world all over again."

—*Kim Barnes*

"Brenda Miller explores the blurred edges between the physical and the spiritual, probes the connective tissues of magnetism, memory, and mysticism. . . . She seamlessly fashions an aesthetic in which the human body can be solidly aware of the moment even as it is 'soaring on the verge of flight.'"

—*Judith Kitchen*

"Miller shows us that a love of language is not merely the province of the poet, but that in the hands of a skillful and original prose writer, the essay becomes, in its own fashion, an ode, an elegy, a sonnet, a sestina."

—*Robin Hemley*

"Brenda Miller continues to do what Brenda Miller always does: make the ordinary extraordinary. . . . In these beautifully composed essays, Miller explores, digs, meditates on what it means to be a woman in this world, to be alive and breathing."

—*Ira Sukrungruang*

ALSO BY BRENDA MILLER

Season of the Body: Essays

Blessing of the Animals

Listening Against the Stone: New and Selected Essays

Who You Will Become

∾

The Pen and the Bell: Mindful Writing in a Busy World
co-authored with Holly J. Hughes

Tell it Slant: Creating, Refining, and Publishing Creative Nonfiction
co-authored with Suzanne Paola

AN EARLIER LIFE

BRENDA MILLER

JUDITH KITCHEN'S
OVENBIRD BOOKS, 2016
PORT TOWNSEND, WA

Judith Kitchen's Ovenbird Books promotes innovative,
imaginative, experimental works of creative nonfiction.

Cover art: "Ghost Deer" by Janet Fagan

Cover and interior design: Ellie A. Rogers

Author photograph: Anita K. Boyle

Library of Congress Cataloging-in-Publication Data is on file.

ISBN: 1-940906-01-6

ISBN-13: 978-1-940906-01-0

CONTENTS

The Woman Who Won't Look Away: An Introduction   ix

An Earlier Life   3

Part I

Who You Will Become   7

L'Chaim   10

Change   12

Impressions   14

In Orbit   16

Spin Art   18

Dark Angel   20

The Physics of Angular Momentum   25

Dress Code   28

Tender   39

Part II

Swerve   51

Pantoum for 1979   52

Aftershocks   55

Scar   57

Giving Your Body to Science   58

Operation   60

Sweat Lodge   61

Wild Mushrooms   64

Headache   66

Groceries   67

Beloved   69

Bright Angel   73

Quite a Storm 76

Box Canyon 78

Altered Fruit 79

Understand 82

Part III

Regeneration 87

Gizzards 92

36 Holes 94

Crush 105

How to Get Ready for Bed 106

Be More 114

The Single Girl's Guide to Remodeling 118

Full Service 134

Greyhound 137

The Rest of the Story 139

Surface Tension 142

To Live For 150

Epilogue

We Regret to Inform You 155

Acknowledgments 173

Notes 174

The Woman Who Won't Look Away: An Introduction

I am honored and delighted to introduce the newest member of the Ovenbird family, even though she's already widely known. Readers familiar with Brenda Miller's wonderful essays will find this collection, chosen and carefully ordered by the author, something new to savor. Anyone still unacquainted with her much-honored work will be in for a special pleasure. It's not just the distinctive voice, candid self-confrontation, or profusion of vividly realized moments and images that make these pieces indelible in the mind and heart. In a word, it's the writing. *Writing.* That loaded term—which we somehow either take for granted or make precious—here reclaims the genuine eloquence of art.

An Earlier Life represents what Ovenbird founder Judith Kitchen envisioned as literary nonfiction at its best: personal, challenging, engaging, and inventive, not by creating "facts" the way a novelist does, but by devising means to sift and shape the memories and moments that make up an individual life in order to open layers of truth that matter to all of us. This is a delicate, unpretentious art, an art of proportion, where truth is more than imagination and style is more than surface affectation. It requires skill and tact and attention, and a kind of wisdom that holds the self in balance, the way time does.

An Earlier Life is intimate, sensuous, kinetic, risky. The personal geography it portrays is as large as Arizona and Alaska; its itinerary to the past bends time and space like a physicist probing new dimensions. Miller possesses a rare ability to re-discover, re-inhabit, re-evaluate who she has been in the light of who she has become, while maintaining the vitality of all these identities. She spins the kaleidoscope of time without losing her own sharp angle of vision, and we time-travel with her. From the ambivalent initiations of girlhood to passionate and painful explorations of relationship, from joyous and joyless embodiment to the longing for bodiless transcendence, these essays illuminate the rifts and seams in our lives. They evoke the incompletion that defines us, the strength that sustains us as we define ourselves.

For all its rueful awareness of consequence and costs, there's an almost impossible tenderness running throughout. The dominant mode is irony, but irony as understanding. How not to be ironic when the persistent theme is a woman's desire to connect and the failure to do so, which every thinking person experiences?

In "Dress Code," Miller lays out a continuum running from First Grade through the many spoken and unspoken codes that define her later youth and adulthood. These enforced masks that promise participation in the world are countered by the need to stabilize an always elusive self. The search for authenticity—the tension between promise and reality, conformity and freedom—is rendered with nuanced and increasingly desperate wit. Seeking "an undress code," the author finds herself spending four years in a "hippie resort in the Mendocino Hills," leading to an incandescent passage (one of many in the book) in which self-discovery and self-negation become one:

*When you're naked, you still feel clothed. You sit at the
edge of the swimming pool, one foot lazily stirring the
body-temperature water. You steam yourself in the sauna,
simmer in the hot tub, until you feel closer to naked, your
personas melting away one by one, until there's nothing
left but a core that burns.*

The book's Epilogue, "We Regret to Inform You," is a droll
catalog of rejection letters covering nearly every phase of Miller's
developing identity. It's as entertaining a performance as something a brilliant conceptual comedian might give—only braver
and far more telling. In place of the self-pity found in some con-
temporary memoir, this essay offers a deadpan contemplation of
inner turmoil that is itself a kind of triumph.

An Earlier Life is a triumphant book. In the brief, riveting essay,
"Understand," Miller walks an Alaskan beach alone at midnight.
Far from home, she finds herself:

*You understand the action of the sea. You feel the sea's
attention on you, a woman who won't look away.*

Brenda Miller is the woman who won't look away. Reader, prepare
to be taken closer to your own life's hidden fire.

Stan Sanvel Rubin
Executive Editor
Judith Kitchen's Ovenbird Books
February 2, 2016

AN EARLIER LIFE

BRENDA MILLER

An Earlier Life

In an earlier life I was a baker, in a bakery on a cobblestoned street. I woke early, in the dark, to do my work. Before the birds. Before the music of the world commenced. In the quiet, I brought something to life. I proofed yeast in large bowls, or I coddled the sourdough mother, urging it to grow. I heard only the scrape of my spoon; I smelled only yeast and flour, honey and egg. My wrists were strong. My back, strong. I knocked a Morse code on the undersides of loaves to test if they were done. Children pressed their noses to the glass, begged for small morsels to fill their mouths. I made special loaves for them, swirled in cinnamon and sugar. It was my only kindness.

PART I

Who You Will Become

*S**halom*: A Hebrew word that means many things at once: hello, goodbye, welcome, peace, and good. In southern California, far from her hometown of Brooklyn, my mother found a Judaica store and bought a hanging *Shalom* sign: bright green Hebrew letters dangled cockeyed from a dove carrying an olive branch. She hung this emblem in the front hallway, across from the formal front door we hardly ever used, so this declaration of *hello, goodbye, welcome, peace,* and *good* greeted strangers—people who didn't know us well enough to use the side door through the garage. I saw it on my way to and from my parents' bathroom or when I opened the door for a friend too shy to barge in through the kitchen. It hung there for years and years, proclaiming its mute offer of welcome.

Shabbat Shalom, we said to our neighbors in the synagogue, my father and brothers wearing their *kippas* bobby-pinned to their heads. *Shabbat Shalom*: a good Sabbath to you, may your family live in peace. We said this easily to one another, and did not speak of what might disturb that peace. *Shabbat Shalom*, we whispered: the "shush" sound of comfort, the open vowel of "om," like the chants I'll sing in yoga class years later—all those syllables the same, washing over us where we sit in half-lotus, our bodies hallowed by sound.

In Hebrew, the word for God means, "I am what I am becoming." This presence is always immanent, always evolving. When we

7

say *Shalom*, we are in the midst of this transition: hello, goodbye, turning to face the past and future at once.

❧

My father mows the lawn in his shorts—shirt off, sneakers stained with grass. Sweat beads on his forehead, glistens between his shoulder blades. His chin is sharp, the cheekbones high, like mine. The relatives always say, *It's easy to see you're daddy's girl, you look just like your father.* I'm watching him from behind the screen door, the mesh dim, as if he's already an old photograph of himself. Sometimes the lawn mower sputters to a stop, and he leans down, pulls the rope with a jerk to start it—such a primitive motion, with its own kind of grace, a man setting the gears in motion with strength and patience. It never starts on the first pull or the second, but sometimes the third will lead to a hopeful sputter, then the fourth tug roars the engine to life.

The air smells of gasoline and cut grass, oranges and iced tea. My father pushes the lawn mower back and forth, creating long furrowed patches of neat grass, taming the unruly blades into mown and obedient lines, the way my mother does with the vacuum cleaner, our shag carpet showing so clearly where it has been cleaned and where it is has not.

I am the unruly child. I try to stay tame, but something in me keeps misfiring. I'm unhappy. I sulk, I slam doors, rattling the *Shalom* in the entry. Later, I will leave a note on my bed for my cousin, but my mother will find it; she'll read how I'm *stoned out of my mind*, and they'll both watch me leave the house with boys so reckless they must hold their breaths until I come home.

But even then I want to feel the peace of a vacuumed house. I want to feel smooth and even as the mown lawn. I want to know the cool satisfaction of a glass of Lipton Iced Tea—with that bitter hint of lemon—after an afternoon of hard work, my parents in their mesh lawn chairs next to the Doughboy swimming pool. I want to know the deep bass comfort of *Shalom*. Why is it so hard? I watch my father while he is mowing, my mother while she is vacuuming; I move from room to room and look out various windows—the noise of the mower, the noise of the vacuum, drowning out any possibility of questions, or answers.

I'll stand in the newly-shorn yard and breathe, alone after a sudden rain. Breathing in the smell of wet pavement, wet metal on the jungle gym, chlorine, eucalyptus. No one knows I'm out here; for a few moments, I do not exist clearly in anyone's mind. I am not a daughter, not a sister, not a friend. I am only a girl standing in a yard. I wear my purple rubber boots.

My dog Sheba galumphs across the sodden grass, stops and looks at me. I raise my arms, and she gallops over. I curve my body across her back and breathe in her wet dog smell, clutch the skin of her neck, and whisper something in her ear. Maybe: *Who's a good girl? Are you a good girl?* We stand in the yard and breathe. We have nowhere to go and everywhere to go. The puddles wink back. They tell me, *Shalom*: hello, goodbye, peace. The eucalyptus say, *Simmer down.* They say: *Become who you will become.*

L'Chaim

When I was eighteen years old, my parents gave me a gold *Chai* necklace—the Hebrew character for eighteen, but also the symbol for life. We toast *L'Chaim!* ("to life!") at every opportunity. I wore it on a gold chain so the pendant fell just between my collarbones. In those days my skin was smooth, tanned dark from constant trips to the Santa Monica beach where we dug ourselves shallow trenches in the sand to lie in like corpses—the sun not gold, exactly, but a stark and dusty yellow, glaring off the dirty shore. The Pacific seemed lazy at that particular strand of beach, the breakers rolling in and rolling out, body surfers rolling harmlessly off their boards; the bigger breakers roiled further north, in Malibu and beyond; that's where we'd go if we wanted to glimpse those surfer boys, with their long legs and shaggy hair, those smiles that could disarm us in an instant.

But most often we stayed in Santa Monica, and we oiled each other up so that our bodies would glow. I took off the necklace then, so it wouldn't burn its symbol into my chest, but otherwise I wore it all the time—even to bed, where I felt the flat gold of *chai* on my skin, a sheen of dampness there, as if the *Chai* itself sweated, and my heart beat against it, lifting up this symbol for life, for eighteen, in little swells.

Though I no longer attended synagogue, I worshipped being eighteen, being alive, in my own way: going to the Mulholland hills with boys, and we smoked and talked and grew silent, lay back on the big boulders and watched the sky, watched the stars come out. We sang songs by Buffalo Springfield, Neil Young, or Fleetwood Mac. We'd all be a little sunburned and have sand in our hair, and we'd all be starving for Winchell's donuts on our way back home at midnight, gliding off the deserted freeway into the Valley, the Winchell's stand lit up like a shrine.

We tumbled through the doors, squinting in the fluorescence, bent down to peruse the crullers and the twists and the glazed. Always I got a buttermilk old-fashioned chocolate, with its hard light shell on the outside and its cakey inside, a flavor I'd give anything to taste again: that first bite in a parking lot, in the summer night, my shorts brushing my thighs, my gold *Chai* gleaming as I swallow. The boy I love leans into me as we lie on the hood of a car that's taken us everywhere we need to go. We'll climb back into that car and drive carefully through the quiet streets until we arrive at my house—the long front window dark, every room dark—and we'll kiss long and hard, our mouths sweet, my parents sleeping inside—or not sleeping, lying awake, praying for the glint of *chai* at my throat, waiting for me to teeter through the door, *Shalom* chiming in my wake.

Change

Friday night: cars nose out of parking lots, moving slowly, kids hanging out the windows and yelling, horns honking; cheerleaders bounce in their boyfriends' letter jackets, while Highland Dancers slip out of their dancing shoes and into heels. My friends and I light up joints before we pile into a beat-up Ford Mustang and head to Bob's Big Boy.

Jolly fat Bob in his checkered hat: two stories high and lit up like a demon, one hand holding a platter of burgers, saying *come in, come in* (years later someone will steal Bob, though it's impossible to imagine how they pulled it off, and where they would have put him and why, this freakish boy-man offering you burgers round the clock), but for now we pull into the parking lot and pat Bob's plastic belly as we tumble into the restaurant. We're a scruffy lot talking too loudly, jostling six of us into one booth. The poor waitress assigned to us wearily sighs and brings our menus, though we don't need menus: all we want are Cokes and fries and a big side order of hot fudge in a bowl.

The waitress rolls her eyes, writes it down, brings our adolescent order to the cook who doesn't care, who's seen it all, and he throws the frozen fries in the day-old grease that bubbles and spits. He wipes his oily forehead with the back of his hand and cocks one hip against the counter. He lifts the fries from the cooker and salts them liberally, ladles the hot fudge into a soup bowl, and the waitress bears this offering back to us, slaps it down, pads away in her thick-soled sneakers, and wipes her hands on her checkered apron. She knows she won't get a tip, or if she does, it will be insulting—a few pennies—so she moves on to the next table, her pen poised above her pad.

We know we'll never end up like *her*: a middle-aged waitress in a chain restaurant on a Friday night, the lights always too bright, the air thick with grease and smoke and the smell of teenagers with their hormones, their pot reek, their braying laughs. No, we'll never end up like *her* (though she was likely no more than a few years older than us), with her weariness, her responsibilities, her shit job. We're smart and we know we'll get out of here, do something else, be something else—but for now we grab the French fries and drag them one by one through the hot fudge, put them in our mouths to crunch the salt and grease and sweet all at once, then wash it down with the astringent tang of Coke.

For now our bodies are just one big craving, only satisfied by this particular combination: not only the fries and hot fudge, but the bodies nestled around us, the elbows and knees and too-long hair, the flash of an eye, the touch of a thigh, the sense of being cocooned with a coven of friends who don't really know you. They know only the self that goes along for the ride, who's grateful to be included, who eats food that makes her ill, who keeps looking at her watch, knowing she should get home.

Eventually we've finished off the fries and hot fudge; only crumpled napkins remain, and smears of chocolate on the paper place mats. A map shows us all the places in the southland we can go for Bob's fluorescent welcome, and we tumble out of the booth, all of us scrounging for change.

Impressions

The classroom smells of wet clay and chalk, and you're in your art smock spattered with tempera paints. The clay is one wet hunk on the table, and the other kids go at it, tearing off chunks, rolling them into balls. But you just touch it with one finger, make a dent in it with your thumb, then the whole hand, a handprint in the cool mass, like the handprints you made in concrete around the swimming pool—your father kneeling with you as you pressed one hand into the sticky cool surface, the suction as you pulled away. Your father scratched in your name, and a date. Then your brothers did it too, and you were instructed to stand back, not to disturb the concrete as the markings dried (though the desire to disturb was strong).

In all the summers to come, as you clambered up the ladder to the little diving board, your hands tugging on your swimsuit bottoms, you passed by those handprints; sometimes you saw them and sometimes you didn't, but always they waved at you from the past.

The clay reminds you of the impressions at the orthodontist's office, the trays filled with a sticky green chalky cement. They clamped those trays over your upper and lower teeth, held your jaw shut, and the cement oozed out the sides. You had to sit very still, keep your mouth shut tight, breathe through your nose, or else they'd have to do it all over again. So you did what you could—

you panted like a frightened horse through your nose. When they finally let you open your mouth, you stretched your neck, implored them to *take it out, take it out*, and afterward you sat back in the huge chair, your eyes closed, tears leaking out the corners of your eyes.

Before too long the orthodontist returned with a perfect replica of your teeth, crooked and ugly, but fascinating nonetheless, and he pointed out where they would fix everything, make your smile beautiful. Afterward, he gave you a set of your impressions to take home with you to keep in a drawer. Every so often you like to run your fingers across the inside of this duplicate mouth with its crooked imperfections.

So now you sit with this lump of wet clay in front of you, wearing your stiff and dirty smock, and you want to mold that clay into something that will last—something that will speak to you from the past, or wave to you a long time. You want something that will remain when your body has changed, sloughed off, but such a thing, you know, is impossible. You know that what will emerge from your hands could never be that beautiful, or that durable, and so you don't want to even try.

But the teacher's looking at you; you have to do something. So you obliterate your handprint and turn the little lump of clay into a bowl, a crooked bowl your mother will profess to love. She'll put it on the counter to hold something valuable: the car keys, or spare change, or perhaps some pieces of artificial fruit.

In Orbit

July 20, 1969: I'm running in a wide circle at the far end of the cul-de-sac, around and around, until I settle in the dust under a thorny bush—but then my name floats into the game of hide-and-seek, calling me back as dusk descends on the neighborhood. Other names unfurl like ribbons, doors opening and closing— *Bobby, Brenda, Laura!*—and none of us kids even says goodbye, we just disperse, our small band so easily dissolved. I leave my perfect hiding place—knees scratched, hair smelling of sap—to go back inside, where it's too hot and smells of stuffed cabbage, the television on to the evening news. Walter Cronkite, his bass voice so reassuring as he tells us that man has gone on an adventure to escape his familiar planet. Father, mother, brothers—we're all angled toward the television because something momentous is about to happen: the first man to walk on the moon.

Somehow we're going to see it. We'll see Armstrong in his space suit emerging from the spaceship's door; we'll see him as if looking through a scratched and dirty window, with blips and bleeps and static, a shimmering gray overlaying every-thing because he's out there now, a lone man in a different atmosphere altogether, moving backward down the ladder one slow step at a time. Just before his foot touches down in the dust, he speaks the words that will become an emblem: *One small step for man, one giant leap for mankind.* And then he does it, takes a little hop down onto that alien surface, the only man in the universe.

Everyone sits quietly watching, forks in midair—I can see the profile of my father's jaw, my mother's small shoulders—and just at that moment, I decide to clank my fork on the edge of my plate, to make a loud noise that will penetrate the vast silence in which this man now moves. Everyone turns toward me: father, mother, brothers (I can imagine even Walter Cronkite, taking off his big black glasses the way he does when he's about to cry) angry, annoyed, and my father says, *Well, thank you very much*, and I know I've ruined it, this historic moment.

I don't know why I did it: maybe I just felt vastly lonely and wanted to make my presence known, or maybe I thought it would be funny, or maybe I was kind of applauding, the way the men in Houston must have been jumping up and down, shaking hands, *mission accomplished* after so many years of study and work and planning, they had *done it*, they had put a man on the moon! My faux pas hangs in the air, the clank of the fork still hurting my ears. They turn back to the television, the set of their bodies so solidly against me, and I guess I don't really understand why it would be so great—to be a man on the moon, exiled, in orbit so far from home.

Spin Art

I'm spinning in a circle—five years old—in the backyard of that Amestoy Avenue house. Alone, save for the eucalyptus trees, still young and thin, watching in their soldierly line, and the orange trees, the grapefruit. The walnut tree too, with its fuzzy covered fruits. I'm spinning and spinning, arms flung out wide, feet in dirty red Keds, the lawn dry and almost green.

Anything that spins has, paradoxically, at its core, something quite still. Something spinning whirls in on itself, but at the same time shoots energy outward. A spinning thing—like a *dreidel*—never knows where it will land. It must acquiesce to the force of orbit. A spinning thing is isolated and connected at once.

I'm spinning and thinking of the carnival at the synagogue, walking among the games of chance until I arrive at the Spin Art machine, all the colors aligned in squeeze bottles like ketchup, while the canvas spins on its peg, so fast it's only a blur, and your job is all timing and finesse: knowing when to squirt in a bit of red, a glob of yellow. The machine itself has no intention; it's all action, all centrifugal force. *Centrifugal*, I learn years later, means "to flee the center," and that's what these colors do once thrown into the mix.

My job is patience. My job is quiet. My job is to go into the center of it without flinching, holding a color in each hand, waiting for the art to arrive. You can't see it while it's still spinning—the art hidden within motion. It will surprise or disappoint; you can't know ahead of time. Spin art is all about the unexpected. About what will be revealed once the spinning stops. Your own blueprint of the universe.

I'm spinning, and any minute now I'm going to fall down laughing, though there's no one to share the joke. But I know someone might be watching: my mother behind the sliding glass door or even from, perhaps, the kitchen, where surely she can't see me but can watch nonetheless. Or something else—as invisible as my mother and as present—that keeps me always in sight, a force that nudges beauty out of chaos.

I'll fall down, laughing, and for a moment feel the way the eucalyptus must feel always: how movement never ceases. I'll hear the laughter of other children nearby; they're close and yet so far. All I have to do is open the gate to join them.

Dark Angel

Pass Over

At Passover, we yell out the plagues with glee—*Blood! Frogs! Vermin!*
We fingerprint wine onto our plates to suggest drops of blood. Eat
little sandwiches made of matzo, brisket, glazed carrots, *haroset* of
chopped apple and pecans. A splash of wine in everything. The
Seder plate in the center of the table: a dish of salt water for tears.

Passover means the angel of death passed over, decided not to
smite. This is what it means to be chosen, to be spared.

Still, at Passover every year I look up, try to see the angel fluttering overhead. I want to see how quickly the choice is made: to
smite or not to smite. The angel looks at me to decide. She tells
me I can choose: how to pass over and leave ourselves unharmed.
It takes a kind of diligence. How easy it is to fall asleep, to forget
the mark of protection, to let the dark angel in.

Milk

You think of them as you eat your cereal. You can't help it; their
faces adorn the cartons. Milk. You never liked milk anyway, it gives
you a stomachache, and now this? A kid who just looks like a kid
on picture day at school, wearing something pretty, gazing off to

the side at something unknown. That kid probably sat just as you do now, head close to the cereal bowl, milk dripping off her lips.

Who thought this was a good idea? Sure, the mothers would frown at them as they set out breakfast, and children would see them through bleary morning eyes. But would we really find them, the MISSING? If you weren't careful, if you forgot to block the milk carton with your cereal box, the MISSING stared at you all through breakfast. They would say, *LAST SEEN*. They would say, *WEARING A BLUE JACKET* (just like yours). They would say, *AGE AT ABDUCTION*. They would say, *AGED PHOTO—NOW 13 YEARS OLD*. They would say, *LAST SEEN WITH*.

They say, *BE CAREFUL*. They say, *I WAS CAREFUL*.

You eat your Cocoa Puffs. Your mother washes the dishes, puts away the missing children. The kitchen window lets in light. Cars cruise up, then down, the cul-de-sac. Cul-de-sacs, they say, are safer. There's no way through. Harder to escape with a child.

Your stomach's upset, but you have to go to school anyway. You have to put on your blue jacket. You have to put on your stiff shoes. You have to walk alone down Amestoy and up Mayall, the long blocks to Andasol Avenue. You try not to think of the MISSING, but they accompany you anyway, scratch a fingernail between your shoulder blades.

You wonder what it's like in the land of the MISSING. You imagine fog. A scent of musty rose. You imagine that to be in the land of the MISSING is to feel one notch higher on the pain scale, something one can measure in the doctor's office. *Tell me*, he asks, *do you feel pain here? Or here?* And when you shake your head he gives you a lollipop, tells your mother there's nothing wrong with you, *She's just a little high strung.*

High strung, words that make you feel pulled taut. Your mother's relieved. She puts her hand on your head, brings you home to drink chocolate milk, which gives you a stomachache. Makes you think of those posters of the horrible diseases you can catch if you don't get vaccinated: measles, mumps, whooping cough. Those cartoon figures writhing in pain.

The next day, the same. Waking is fine for a few minutes. But then the MISSING stare at you. They wander around with their aged photographs, growing up in absentia. Here they are at age six, age ten, age thirteen. You believe the MISSING must hold those photos and gaze at them fondly. You imagine they must have something to say. You wonder if they recognize themselves. You wonder if they recognize each other out there in the world, one missing child nodding to another.

Lifeguard

White glare of the sun on the beach: it's always too much, this heat rising, and we lie on our backs, in our bikinis, bellies glistening, thighs glistening, anything that could glisten glistening. Our bodies reflect back the sun so the whole beach seems colonized by slick tongues of light. All of us squint when we rise up on our elbows to watch the surfer boys, or to look sideways at the lifeguard on his station; we always set up next to the same tower, #15, and the boy there with his sandy blond hair, the same wispy strands on his muscular calves. His shorts hang down to the knee, a worn elastic waistband hugging his slim torso—hardly any hips at all to keep them up, it would take just the lightest teasing tug to bring them down—and he casually holds the life ring, his foot up on the rails, sunglasses hiding his eyes.

He never notices us, makes it a *point* not to notice us: girls who glisten and glisten for him. He keeps his eyes trained on the ocean—*our* ocean, the ocean we've known our entire lives—to see any signs of distress among the children who build sand castles at the very edge of the tide, or the older kids who run face-first into the waves, or the grandmothers in their skirted swimsuits and varicose veins, standing with their white toes in the water, or the young men and women who dive beyond the breakers where the sea rises and falls in gentle swells, or the ones who actually *swim* in that water, as if in a pool, the Australian crawl, arm over arm, or the backstroke, going out a little farther, a little farther . . .

We sometimes lazily rise to our feet, make our way past the calm lick of the tide, into the breaking point, timing our dives into a curl, enduring that moment when it's all foam and chaos, then bobbing up, safe, on the other side, where it's very quiet, the waves already distant, a muted rumble. We dog paddle and look back to find our blanket next to tower #15, and we see the life-guard scanning the middle distance; we see glistening feet, and children in swim trunks with dripping ice cream cones, mothers reading magazines, the pages flipping steady as a metronome. We turn and swim toward open ocean, the current carrying us north, toward the pier where there's a Ferris wheel and corn dogs, and soda pop, and games of chance.

We always flip on our backs and drift just a minute—ears just under the surface, eyes open to the dim blue of the sky, hips bobbing in the restless water—but then we come to with a start, turn around and see how far we've drifted. It's a dog paddle that morphs into an Australian crawl, but we're not getting very far, and we can see the lifeguard stand up now, his gaze zeroed in, the whistle in his lips (those lips we've imagined kissing oh so many times); he's ready to blow, and we see his skinny legs, see that he's not really very old, just a kid really, like us, how could he save anyone? And we kick and kick toward shore, the current lessening, a swell coming up from behind to take us all the way in.

We're now among unfamiliar blankets and sand castles, old men in Speedos, their bellies red, their knees white—but we can see our way back, we can see the lifeguard sit down, arms crossed over his hairless chest, the life ring tapping against his knee; we can see our blanket and our tanning oils and the cooler full of tuna sandwiches our mothers made us so long ago. Salt begins drying on our faces, tightens them into masks of summer. Sand massages the arches of our feet, and we feel so tired, more tired than we've ever been in our lives, as we make our way back to tower #15, where the lifeguard keeps his gaze neutrally on the sea, though we think we can see a scowl now shading the fine hair on his upper lip.

He's watching again for any sign of distress. We want to show him how distress takes many forms—sometimes not so obvious—and that we all need saving, every day. We want to climb up there with him, offer him a lemonade, the glass sweating in our hands, and sit with our thighs barely touching his while the sun glares down, then gentles in a breeze—turns into one of those green, dirty sunsets we love so much, the only kind of beauty we've known.

The Physics of Angular Momentum

Any two objects that pass one another will naturally begin to spin. Here, at the Grateful Dead show, you've become a physics experiment, your body gaining momentum from each body you encounter. Bodies thin and dry; bodies heavy and damp. Half-naked bodies and bodies swathed in scarves. Bodies that have flown off their handles—arms wild, bodies unnaturally arched.

You're all spinning off one another, flinging off layers like a truck tire losing its tread on the highway: big hard pieces littering the road, hazardous, until you're down to bare rubber and flying. Those Sufi whirling dervishes knew the most direct way in to God is via a circle—you can't get there in a straight line, as the crow flies. All this spinning shears off the crust that keeps you separate from each other, and now you're all merging until the music stops.

But even then you keep spinning, out the door to the bathroom, where all those bodies that seemed so beautiful on the dance floor now look bedraggled in the fluorescent light: lips chapped, feet filthy, pupils too dark in pale faces, skin clammy. You catch a sideways glimpse of yourself in the mirror—thin, gaunt, your hair in strings along your face—until someone pulls you from the mirror, says gently, *Don't look too long, man.* You spin back out into the crowd that's circling the stadium, a surge, and you enter that current.

Two selves: that person in the mirror, ghastly yet fascinating, and the other self who merges with the crowd, without body or the concept of a body. Something you'll understand soberly years later, as you sit in a meditation group and sing the "Heart of the Prajñāpāramitā": a chant you can't understand with your mind: *no body, no form, no tongue, no eyes, no cause of ill-being, no end of ill-being, and no path.* Then you'll walk slowly in a circle around the cushions, one foot in front of the other, a body that's constantly in flux and going away.

You'll sit in the meditation hall with a hundred others, watching the breath on its curious journey through the body, and then it will all shift: instead of you breathing air, the air will breathe you. You feel it most strongly in the gaps between inhale and exhale, between exhale and inhale, the lull at the dome of each one; you'll understand, for a brief moment, how your lungs, your heart, are ferocious—a force that has nothing at all to do with you. You'll feel the buoyancy of your heart on the repeating waves of the breath, before you come back to this solid world of the body in its habitat, the mind certain that it needs to intervene to survive.

But for now you're in this tribe of Deadheads who take LSD like medicine that might cure you of the disorder of simply being alive in the world at age twenty and twenty-one and twenty-two, the skin of your minds so tender. Afterward, you were *fried*: your mouths dry, skin pale, shuffling those bodies that now seemed heavier than before. You guzzled down quarts of orange juice to try to replenish, smoking hand-rolled cigarettes in the van, gazing out the window at the rain, the songs still unspooling in your minds—*and it's just a box of rain*—just whispers now, the rhythm beating softly in your blood.

And already you started planning for the next Dead show, where you could leave those tired, so ordinary bodies behind: to peel away, like the eucalyptus trees you loved as a child, the way they seemed unmoved, unchanged in the backyard, the row of them like sentinels against the high fence. The word *eucalyptus* means "sufficiently covered"—the buds, the seeds, the flowers— while the trunk of the tree is all about *uncovering*: stripping away. When you scrambled up among them, lifting yourself onto the berm, you found long sheets of their bark: tough and fibrous, light and heavy at once. The trunks smelled bright, fresh, continually shedding what they no longer need.

Dress Code

First Grade

You must wear something clean. You must wear clothing that matches even a little bit—some hint that the colors are *trying* to coordinate. Yes, we know you can dress yourself, but you must wear shoes. You must wear socks with those shoes, preferably two that match. You must not show your underpants, but if you do, accidentally—as you are prone to do when lost in the spiral of the carousel or the wide momentum of the swing (which you always insist on swinging high, too high, to the very edge of the acceptable arc)—these underpants should not be dirty. Dirty underpants bring shame upon you. And upon your poor mother, and your mother's mother, a shame going back generations to the field in Tasmania, where—although these women were poor and had little they could call their own—they still knew how to keep their underpants clean. Why can't you keep your underpants clean? What is wrong with you?

Third Grade

You must wear a green corduroy jumper that's too heavy for the weather, and you must wear green-striped knee socks that do not slump to your ankles. If you do have knee socks that slump to your ankles, at least have clean kneecaps, pink and unscabbed. If you can't manage even that, you are a shame upon yourself and your mother and your mother's mother. Do not cut your hair above the ears. If, by mistake, you do cut your hair above the ears, be prepared for the taunts: *You look like a boy! You look like a boy!* Be prepared for the one that hurts the most, the one hissed by your best friend as she stands a few inches behind you in line, her face half-turned to the other girls to get their approval. Her hiss will be like a dart entering just under the breastbone.

Sixth Grade

For sixth grade graduation, you must wear a pale blue dress with puffed short sleeves and an empire waist, so that you resemble, quite closely, a parade float: the kind you've seen on television on Thanksgiving Day. All you need is a string tied to your hips and a motorcar slowly dragging you down Fifth Avenue. You must wear white pantyhose that sag at the knees, and white patent leather shoes that pinch at the toes. These shoes are impossible to keep clean, but you must keep them clean, at least for the duration of the ceremony. But they smudge the second you walk out of the house— what is wrong with you? Now all the pictures will be marred by dirt. You will stand flanked by your best friends, whose dresses are pale yellow, whose hair is combed neatly, whose smiles are never forced.

Seventh Grade

You must wear a sweater to the first day of junior high, Patrick Junior High, even though the temperature is in the high eighties.

Don't change, even if you're already sweating in your bedroom. *Don't Change.* That's what the signatures in your grammar school yearbook told you: *Don't Change. See you next year!* So you don't change. You must be determined to stay the way you are, forever. So you wear the sweater—the one you bought especially for the first day of school, because in the air-conditioned dressing room it felt so soft against your skin, and that green so pretty against your eyes—and it will make you so hot you'll throw up on the grass after your mother parks the car.

An inauspicious beginning to junior high, to this school named after a patriot who famously cried, *Give me liberty or give me death!* All the students fidget against their restraints and spend nearly every class hour yearning to be free. You won't know it until years later, but Patrick Henry not so famously had a wife who went insane. When she became dangerously disturbed she was "clothed in a Quaker Shirt," precursor to the straitjacket. You've never been in a straitjacket but imagine it many times, how it would feel to be so swaddled you could harm neither yourself nor others.

You'll think of Sarah, Patrick Henry's wife, and her six children, and the Quaker Shirt tight against her shoulder blades. She will live the rest of her life in a basement apartment, tended to by her loving husband, a man who knows something about restraints. You will try to imagine such love, how it wraps around a person—not like a Quaker Shirt, but a heavy terry cloth robe, white and oh-so-clean.

Tenth Grade

You must be preoccupied with uniforms. You will watch movies of girls in boarding school and crave their crisp khaki skirts, their pressed white blouses, the little kerchiefs knotted neatly at the throat. You will study pictures of women in uniform—stewardesses, waitresses, nurses—and envy even the utilitarian shoes with their thick soles. Ah, to be freed from the tyranny of the closet! Your closet—which offers up its sad retinue day after day, asking you to choose.

When you enter high school—Granada Hills High—you will set your sights on becoming a Granada Hills Highlander—one of those girls who dress in Scottish costumes and dance the Highland Fling during Friday night football halftimes. They wear plaid kilts and tight fitting waistcoats fastened with hook and eye. They wear black lace-up slippers and white knee socks. They must always smile; the smile is part of the complicated dress code, the Highland Fling a joyful dance, a dance of victory. The dancers all look tall and chiseled and fit; when they dance, their pointed toes cross in front and behind and in front of the opposite knee. The moves are all sanctioned and perfect. There is no improvisation in the Highland Fling.

You practice the Fling in gym class. You must kick out your legs and raise your arms into an arc above your head, your fingertips touching. You smile hard. But your moves are clumsy and imperfect. Your knees pull in at odd angles, your ankles thick and heavy, so you do not fling so much as stomp. Your toes cramp when they point. You won't make even the first cut.

So you set your sights lower—on the "stat girls" who keep score at the basketball games. Their uniform is a simple letter jacket, in green and white leather, which they wear on Friday afternoons no matter the weather. These girls do not have to be tall or fit; they simply have to be observant, and good with numbers, keeping track of stats for each player: the number of rebounds, assists, goals, fouls. They sit in a row just above the players' bench, so they get a clear view of sweaty backs, muscled calves. While the players look to the cheerleaders—in their short pleated skirts, the big H emblazoned on their breasts—behind them the stat girls stare at cute bums in long shorts, take the players' measure in more ways than one.

You take the test, studying stats and percentages, dreaming of that heavy letter jacket and your own clipboard. On the day they announce the stat girl roster over the PA, you're sure your name will be mentioned. You set your face to act surprised, that anticipatory smile on your lips, but when the announcement is over your name remains unsaid. You sit for a few moments with that smile still on your lips, then let it fade as inconspicuously as you can. No one else will really be listening to the announcements; your classmates ignore you in their customary ways, nothing special in their disdain. You'll look down and notice a stain—Orange juice? Jelly?—on your white Keds. You see that your knee socks have once again slumped to your ugly ankles. What is wrong with you?

Twelfth Grade

By this time, you must give up on the idea that you'll be appropriately dressed for the occasion—any occasion. You will get sent home from your job at J.C. Penney for wearing argyle knee socks, though they are clean and do not slump to your ankles. You will go to what someone told you was a costume party, wearing kitten ears and a tail, and at the door all eyes will turn your way as you survey in horror the room full of jeans and t-shirts. We know you're trying. You've tried to follow the dress code, but must have missed the tutorial on the special function of the decoder ring. The one that tells you how to interpret all the changing signs of fashion.

You'll start wearing a lot of plaid, not because you're a thwarted Highland dancer, but because it doesn't show the dirt. You'll shop at Sears with your mother, and buy nothing because nothing fits. You are *between sizes*. For the rest of your life you will be "between sizes," no matter your weight or your level of fitness. It will be as though no size has been devised that conforms to your particular curvature of muscle and bone.

Most of the time, in your clothes, you will feel as though you're trying too hard—even in jeans and a t-shirt—so you pretend to not care, wearing hippie clothes carefully assembled to give the curated pose of not caring. You'll wear baggy shirts, worn-out jeans, halter-tops, or peasant shirts with elastic at the throat and the wrists. This elastic chafes at your skin, leaves small welts that itch and itch. You suffer under this clothing that's designed for comfort.

Later, you'll read about clothing used as various forms of penance: the hair shirt, for instance, woven of goat hair to girdle the loins. You'll feel the shame your ugliness brings upon yourself, and your mother, and your mother's mother. You'll wonder what penance you are serving: you, in your mismatched clothes that hurt.

College

Okay, this casual thing, it's going a bit too far. You'll embarrass your big brother by showing up on campus in dirty overalls and bare feet. What is wrong with you? The sidewalks in Northridge heat up to a hundred degrees; you will hop from foot to foot as you cross the burning asphalt.

You'll make your way north, to Berkeley, where it's cooler and you can wear the ratty sweaters you favor. But the sheer number of hip people frightens you. You get there just in time to hear of Jim Jones—a Bay Area pastor—leading his followers to Africa. Something's not right in the air; people gather in clumps and solemnly shake their heads. You want to understand the desire to follow a leader to your death, to have faith that an afterlife is better than the life you live on earth. You hear a new band, the Talking Heads, in the quad, and something about their music sets you dancing, though you don't really want to dance. You want to cry instead.

You become a Deadhead. Here, the uniform is clear: Fatigued army jacket with swirly skirt. Patches of skulls and roses. Dilated pupils. You take on this uniform easily, and the dancing you do is fluid, all kinetic motion, frantic to fling off anything that binds you to *you*.

Post-Bac

You must find a place that has an "undress code." This place will be Orr Hot Springs, a hippie resort in the Mendocino woods that declares, at the gated entrance, "You may encounter nudity beyond this point." This declaration can be taken as both warning and self-congratulation—a grin.

You'll end up living at this place for four years, and during this time you must be nude for approximately a third of your waking hours. There is nudity in the bathhouse, in the sauna, and in the swimming pool. There is nudity in the communal shower (but no shampoo allowed!). There is nudity on the paths to and from these various areas, though most people put on some form of clothing while cooking dinner in the communal dining room. Still you see many bare breasts dangling over the chopping block, many a naked behind swaying as someone washes the dishes.

During the community meetings, some of the residents show up in bathrobes or towels. You have no money, so you scrounge your outfits out of the Free Box on the porch. The lid of the Free Box is heavy and thick; you have to hold it open with one hand while you rummage with the other. You find large tie-dyed t-shirts, cotton shorts with fringed hems, wrap-around paisley skirts that are not quite threadbare. It's as though the Free Box time traveled from the 1960s, its contents held snug in a treasure chest for you to open. When you're not naked, you'll wear these things like a uniform, sashaying through the lodge with your tanned calves, your strong shoulders.

When you're naked, you still feel clothed. You sit on the edge of the swimming pool, one foot lazily stirring the body-temperature water. You steam yourself in the sauna, simmer in the hot tub, until you feel closer to naked, your personas melting away one by one, until there's nothing left but a core that burns.

Zendo

When you're between sizes, it's tempting to buy pants with elastic waists. There's one pair of pants you can't resist, from Chefwear: your vegetable pants. They are made of a sturdy cotton, with rows of vibrant vegetables running up and down the legs: violet eggplants, pencil-sharp carrots, asparagus shafts, ripe tomatoes, purple cabbage, ears of husked corn. Each of these vegetables stays in its furrowed row, the black field mimicking the fertile earth from which they came.

You will get compliments on these pants, which will keep you wearing them at inappropriate times. You wear them on a meditation retreat, the bright vegetables so vibrant against everyone else's muted brown.

On Buddhist retreats you'll notice, of course, the monks, and the way they can pull off the brown robe draped over a shoulder. At a retreat in the YMCA of the Rockies, you'll see nuns swimming in the pool, still clothed in their raiment, the robes fluttering out behind them like the skin of an otter. Their bald heads shine as bright as their smiles. You know the robes are meant to create a blank field for the true self to emerge. You look down at your vegetable pants and feel a shame that goes back to your mother, and your mother's mother. What is wrong with you?

Yoga Class

After taking yoga classes for twenty years, you must finally advance beyond the beginning class. You take yin yoga, vinyasa yoga, intuitive flow, and feel the way your body has started to adapt to the postures, to *become* them. You take your glasses off so, if there's a mirror in the room, you see only a blurred outline of yourself—hips narrow, shoulders wide. You see this body finding the core of itself in plank, lowering slowly to the belly the way you've been taught, and swooping into upward-facing dog.

It's not until after the class is over that you notice you're wearing dirty sweatpants, smears of your breakfast yogurt decorating the knees. You see the way your tank top has stretched out along the straps, the elastic showing. You envy the younger yoginis and their tight yoga pants that emphasize flat bellies, shapely butts, strong backs.

The Athleta catalog comes in the mail. It always comes in the mail, sometimes two or three times a week, an annoying voice nattering in your ear: *See how these $80 yoga pants will shape you up? See what you could do in this $50 camisole?* The women in these clothes do yoga on stand-up paddleboards. They swing through a Bali marketplace in cute little dresses they've thrown over their yoga clothes. They do downward dog in a desert, or straddle splits atop a horse. On the website, in the "inspiration gallery," they say: *Out here, I'm free. To be me. Ready to take on anything.* You fill your virtual cart with spandex that will let you *be free, to be me,* but then balk at the final price tag this freedom requires.

Sunday School

When you hear the word *becoming* directed, for the first time, at you, you'll flush with pleasure. *That's very becoming,* the saleswoman says as you walk timidly out of the dressing room, and you turn in front of the three-way mirror, seeing parts of yourself you never consider: the back of your head, the indent of your knees. You'll think about the way the word *becoming* means both "attractive" and "emerging." The word for *God,* in Hebrew, means "I am becoming who I will become." When you wear something that fits, you feel yourself *becoming* in all senses of the word.

You'll remember the men in the synagogue, decked out at Rosh Hashanah and Yom Kippur. The men in their fringed prayer shawls, veiled in the name of God. The veil both reveals and conceals, and God hovers both visible and invisible at once. For the devout, God abides in the spaces in between; God is between sizes. Some of the men wear *tefillin*: a small box, strapped to the upper arm, that holds fragments of Torah. These men are clothed in sacred text.

At some point you find yourself in a Quaker meeting, and the silence wraps around you like a robe. Here there is no need to worry about your clothes; no one notices. Traditional Quakers wear "plain dress," so as not to bring attention to worldly things. *Plain*, a word you did your best to avoid as a child. For a while you wore clothes to get attention, then clothes to *not* get attention. Here, you are clothed in silence, a substance that fits you like a glove.

It reminds you of a story your friend Connie told you about working at a preschool in Manhattan. They built a butterfly cage, filled it with monarchs. The children spread sugar water on their arms and legs, then walked inside the chicken wire. The butterflies lit on them by the dozens, sipping at their skin. Some of the children might have cried, some must have laughed, but all, for a few moments, stood clothed in this unearthly gauze, a cloth made wholly of light.

Tender

I

1954. My parents get married. It's a December wedding, a few days shy of Pearl Harbor Day, and my mother is happy for many reasons, but one of them is that, for the honeymoon drive, she gets to wear the new car coat she bought at Best & Co.: a black alpaca that wraps around her body and falls just above the knee.

My mother is twenty years old when she marries. Her hands, as they clutch the car coat closed at her chest, are perfectly manicured, and she's penciled her eyebrows into a cunning arch. There's not a trace of worry in her eyes as she turns to look at the camera, one foot already in the borrowed car. She looks like a rich person, so carefree is her stance, so ready for anything.

My mother and father have courted for about a year, attending many Broadway shows. After they marry, they'll see *Fiddler on the Roof*, with Zero Mostel in the lead, his "If I Were a Rich Man" so popular that you can hear men and women whistling it under their breath as you walk in the garment district, or down the Brooklyn streets lined with brownstones. *If I were a rich man, yididididido* . . . the words trailing off, because you can't even dare say it fully, what you might do with money if you had it.

I imagine the day after the wedding, at their breakfast in a café, my father teaches my mother how to write a check. She's never had a checking account, though she's held her own job since high school, working as a secretary on Madison Avenue. Now she's a married woman; she won't work again for a long time—won't don the business pumps that show off the lovely curve of her ankle, or take the subway from Brooklyn into the city, her manicured nails holding onto the pole as she sways. She liked to window shop on her lunch hour, gazing at the pocketbooks and hats that look so delicious.

My father puts his arm around her, draws her into his side, and shows her the long rectangular packet of checks, with the perforated stubs on the side. He shows her how to write in the date—*There you go, just write it in on that line*—and how to write out the amount in dollars and cents, how to record the transaction on the little stub and keep the balance current. *It's easy*, he says and she nods, but turns the checkbook back over to him to sign, for that last flourish that says, *I'm good for it*.

She waits in the booth while he goes up to pay the bill and then bring the car around; it's cold outside, and the coffee cup is stained with her lipstick, the leftover dregs a little scummy now with cream. He's a good man, with a good job, and they've already been nosing around New Jersey for a suitable place to live, a place within their budget. Like any married woman, she'll have a budget now, a word that seems vaguely ugly, pushy and squat. It's a mystery how a budget might work: the income and outflow and always a little left over for savings.

My young parents are considering a house in a development near Cherry Hill, a name that makes my mother think about trees flowering with abundance, but there are no cherry trees in Cherry Hill. She lights a cigarette and watches my father hurry off to the car, waits for it to float into view like the Staten Island Ferry, ready to take her off, slow but steady, into the rest of her life.

II

1967. I'm eight years old, and I have my own savings account in the Northridge Savings and Loan, a brick building that sits at the far end of the big strip mall a few blocks from home. We spend a lot of time here: shopping at the Hughes super-market, the Sav-On drugstore, Baskin Robbins Ice Cream, the Florsheim shop, and the Hallmark store. But I love especially Delicious Bakery, with its sesame-flecked *challah*, its famous chocolate-chip Danish and seven-layer cakes we take home in pink boxes tied up with string.

The ladies who work the counter wear dirty white aprons knotted in bows just under their enormous breasts, and they wear crinkly white paper bonnets with elastic binding their foreheads, like shower caps. They look mean, but can be surprisingly generous, handing down free butter cookies to shy girls who swing on their mothers' skirts.

These cookies always seem an unexpected bounty, no matter how many times it happens: *Say thank you*, my mother murmurs, and I do: *Thank you*—my voice small in the bustle of the bakery, the women tired, their wrinkles dusted with flour. Their finger-nails are clipped in even lines with the blunt tips of their fingers, which they rest for a moment on the top of the glass counter before turning to the next customer who waves her number tugged from the dispenser at the front of the store, the pink tab with its cut-out little half moon.

Maybe with my savings account I'll be able to wave my own number, buy something of my own at the bakery, something I won't have to share. I understand that you need to *save* money: not only to build up your fortune, but to rescue it—you need to protect your cash from forces that lurk to destroy it.

The Northridge Savings and Loan rests in a shady corner of the shopping center, surrounded by hedges—a little aloof from the other buildings. My brother and I grow hushed as we wait in line with our mother, hemmed in by thick, red velvet ropes. Sometimes she's lugging a bagful of rolled coins—cigar-sized tubes filled with change we've rolled up from the big Best Foods mayonnaise jar that lives on my father's dresser.

We get to wait in line with my mother as long as we stay quiet. I hold tight to the sleek little bankbook they've given me, with its blue leatherette cover, and the green pages inside, so smooth, lined with a precise grid. I take this book out several times a day and hold it in my hands, turning the pages carefully so they remain clean. I have only a few entries so far, each one penciled in by the smiling tellers, deposits written in their careful penmanship, my balance always updated with each turn.

The tellers look entirely perfect, every day, their hair whipped up in lacquered beehives, their fingernails immaculate. They count out withdrawals with crisp authority and know how to lick their thumbs to keep the bills from sticking, though the new tellers wear large rubber thimbles. All of them wear rings that glint below their knuckles. I gape at these women and grow even shyer in their presence, because they seem to me a wholly different breed of female: so confident in the presence of so much money.

Most of the mothers I know are pretty enough, but something about them is slightly askew. They seem to be in a perpetual state of worry, especially when it comes to money; my own mother always looks hesitant when it comes to doling out payments, writing her checks slowly, studying them over the top of her glasses before handing them over to the cashier.

I take any opportunity to make a deposit, just to see those lines in the book accumulate. I keep the passbook in a box on my desk and sometimes stroke it before going to sleep, confusing it, perhaps, with Aladdin's magic lamp. I don't know where my money is, but I imagine it somewhere dim and cool—*saved.*

III

1969. We're in New York City for my brother's bar mitzvah party. Actually it's his *second* reception; the first one happened back home, in the San Fernando Valley, at our own synagogue—Temple Ner Tamid, with its southern Cal breezeways, its ordinary façade of cinder block and plate glass.

My brother did a good job at his ceremony, scowling only a little as he strolled down the center aisle, cradling the velvet-covered Torah in his arms. He hardly made a misstep in his Torah reading, his voice a little high and strained, sure, but at least he *did* it—at least he made it up there in front of all those people, after the literal kicking and screaming that took place at home before the tortured lessons with the rabbi. I hadn't helped either, gloating as I sailed past him while he stepped into the station wagon, me on my pink Schwinn with its flying pink streamers on the handlebars, blessedly free.

It hadn't yet dawned on me that a bar mitzvah meant *money,* lots of it, along with big presents: the kind you get only on the last night of Hanukkah, after all the piddling socks and underwear, the colored pencils and stickers, and then the grand unveiling: the pink Schwinn in the garage, say, or the pair of white leather roller skates. And here it was, mid-summer, and my brother—having proved himself a man—had already raked in a bounty from our California friends, and now we'd flown across the country so our New York kin could similarly fête him.

I'd already been told I wouldn't have a bat mitzvah, because bat mitzvahs weren't mandatory; hardly any of the girls I knew had them because they involved days spent cloistered in the rabbi's office, memorizing Hebrew with its guttural, unlovely inflections. They involved lavish parties that cost our parents a bundle, so when we declined the hesitant offers of studying for bat mitzvah— offers always accompanied by dire warnings of the work involved— we could see the barely-disguised relief flare in their eyes. With boys it was different, especially with first-born sons, especially with first-born sons of California Jewish families, whose ties to the old-school brand of East Coast Judaism had already strained to the point of vanishing.

And so: this extravagant double bar mitzvah for my big brother, who takes it all with incredible nonchalance. It's so *unfair*! No one had told me about all those sleek envelopes lined with cash, or the savings bonds, or the way a person actually grows taller, more polished, under the adoring gaze of one's family.

IV

1972. I'm thirteen years old and aware of Bill French. Very aware of Bill French. At the picnic tables, my girlfriends and I have the sack lunches our mothers packed so carefully—egg salad sandwiches, apples, cookies—but we can't be bothered with them; they are only props, an excuse to be outside where it is warm, and we're wearing tank tops that expose our tanned shoulders. The air feels like a mist of cologne on our skin, the delicate spritz our mothers, when feeling generous, sometimes give us from the mirrored trays on their dressers.

Some of us have lunch boxes instead of bags; some of us even still have cartoon lunch boxes, *The Little Mermaid*, and only now, in the last week, have we realized that we're too old for the little mermaid, whose story ends—in the real version—so sadly, the beautiful mermaid mute, her tongue cut out for love. But we don't remember that part, only remember the beautiful half-woman singing so sweetly above the turbulent waves.

I'm aware of Bill French. He's all freckles and red hair and big hands and square jaw, and I don't know why it's *him*, why I feel so nervous when I glimpse that flicker of hair in the hallway, when I see that freckled nose barreling by. I just know that I need to talk to him. My two girlfriends, Jana and Valentina, flank me, they hold my arms on either side, they're giggling and then hushing as Bill French and his sidekicks approach. He's about to pass by, but pauses, like a buck sensing something in the air, and his head swivels my way, a laugh from a joke told moments before still on his lips.

And then I say it. Fast. *Hey Bill, do you have a quarter I can borrow?* My voice comes out high and strangled. A quarter? Why would I need a quarter? *To get a coke*, I blurt, and he shrugs, digs in his pants pocket, and emerges with the silver coin in hand. Bill French is a nice guy. He'll give you a quarter, sure, why not?

He drops it in my palm, and just as he pulls away his fingers graze mine. The sensation is so intense, so foreign, that my fingers twitch and curl. Then he says, *See ya*, and he goes away, while I clutch the coin tight against my palm. Valentina and Jana are struck dumb; in a moment we'll turn to each other and shriek muffled cries, but for now we're simply waving in the wake of boy passing by—three fronds of sea anemone. I'm left with this warm damp coin in my fist, a token, something I could slip into a machine to get whatever I want.

But I know I won't. I know that instead I'll tuck it in my pocket, bring it home, then slip it into the box with my old bankbook and a sleeve of virgin coins my father bought for me at the U.S. Mint many years ago. It won't be something to spend; this coin will be something to save, an object more than simple tender.

V

1978. I'm eighteen years old and getting ready to leave home for the first time. I'm going to Berkeley, and Berkeley still conjures up images of children gone a little wild amid clouds of patchouli and smoke. It will be a turbulent year for the Bay Area—the preacher, Jim Jones, even at this moment, is leading his followers to their death in South America, and I'll be packing up the Pinto to head into the city, into the thick of it.

But for now I'm in my parents' bedroom, looking at that big jar of coins on my father's dresser. It's stuffed full of pennies mostly, but some dimes, nickels, and quarters glint among the sludge of copper. There might even be a half-dollar buried in the muck.

Ever since I was a little girl I've watched this jar fill up, and then deplete, then fill up again, like the tides; my parents used the money for family trips to Las Vegas, Reno, or for small improvements on the house. My mother spent every Sunday carefully clipping coupons from the paper, arranging them in an envelope, fastening them with paper clips, so that when the time came to pay she could pull this envelope out like an extra bundle of cash. She counted up whatever she saved—a quarter here, a dime there— and put that money in the jar. My father contributed whatever spare change cluttered his pockets at the end of the day.

The bedroom smells of Old Spice and leather shoes and my mother's cologne, White Shoulders, which is like the powder of many flowers in an English garden. And underneath it all, the musty scent of sleep. I touch the jar, put my palm flat against the cold glass. I can see my father's cufflinks, his heavy ring, and his money clip on the lacquered dresser top.

Am I alone in the house? I think my father's in the garage, tinkering with my car. He wants to get me to Berkeley in one piece. My mother is probably out shopping; she's buying me supplies she thinks won't be available in the several cities I'll pass on my way up north. She's wary of Berkeley and its health food stores. The house has that weird silence I'd hear on mornings when I stayed home sick from school; I'd wake from a fevered nap in the middle of the day, the house a family member in its own right, settled on its haunches, keeping watch.

Right now, I want to take this jar, stow it away as a talisman. But I could never ask for it. These days, I don't know how to say anything to my father that doesn't come out angry, or contemptuous, or a complaint. And that jar is something in which they take pride, something they *do*. It's part of their marriage—a clear reliquary that measures the years, collects bits and pieces of the days that make up a life.

The coins would feel cool on my hands if I dug into them, if I poured them out to cover my arms. But they remain stubbornly apart from me, behind the curve of glass. I don't want to steal it—I want my father to simply give me the jar without hesitation. I want him to put it on the passenger seat, the whole thing, and say, *Take it.* The jar would make a little indentation in the upholstery as it settled in for the ride. Perhaps I'd rest a hand on the jar—maybe even buckle it in—to keep this money safe as I make my way so far from home.

PART II

Swerve

I'm sorry about that time I ran over a piece of wood in the road. A pound of marijuana in the trunk and a faulty brake light— any minute the cops might have pulled us over, so you were edgy already, and then I ran over that piece of stray lumber without even slowing down. *Thunk, thunk,* and then the wood spun behind us on the road. Your dark face dimmed even darker, and you didn't yell at first, only turned to look out the window, and I made the second mistake: *What's wrong?* That's when you exploded. *You're so careless, you don't even think. What if there had been a nail in that thing?* you yelled, your face so twisted now, and ugly. *And I'm always the one that cleans it up whenever something breaks.*

I'm sorry, I said, and I said it again, and we continued on our way through the desert, in the dark of night, with the contraband you had put in our trunk, with the brake light you hadn't fixed blinking on and off, me driving because you were too drunk, or too tired, or too depressed, and we traveled for miles into our future, where eventually I would apologize for the eggs being overcooked, and for the price of light bulbs, and for the way the sun blared through our dirty windows and made everything too bright, and I would apologize when I had the music on and when I had it off, I'd say sorry for being in the bathroom, and sorry for crying, and sorry for laughing, I would apologize, finally, for simply being alive, and even now I'm sorry I didn't swerve, I didn't get out of the way.

Pantoum for 1979

I'm twenty years old, barely an adult, my belly flat—though inside that belly a baby is growing. Or not a baby: a *something*, a cluster of cells lodged in the fallopian tubes. In a few weeks I'll be in pain, like a penknife stabbing again and again. But for now I'm just a girl in a broken down Toyota, moving her few belongings into a room in a big red house on the hill.

Not a baby, I'll remind myself later, just a cluster of cells, lodged where it didn't belong. I must have found this house from a tacked message on a bulletin board on campus, an index card with a man's spidery handwriting looking for boarders. For now I'm just a girl, broken down, with few belongings to move into this big red house on the hill. I got the room set apart from all the others, with no windows, in the back.

I must have found this house from a tacked message on a bulletin board, after seeing the run-down hippie pads in Arcata, the cluttered trailer in McKinleyville. This house, in Blue Lake, four miles inland, lies just beyond the fog line that descends on coastal towns. I chose the room set apart: no windows, in the back. The bus runs several times a day and stops just at the foot of this hill.

This house, in Blue Lake lies just beyond the fog line that descends on coastal towns. I'm carrying in some battered boxes of books, a suitcase of clothes, photo albums, a hippie bedspread, some thin pillows. The bus stops with a hiss at the foot of the hill. My new roommate, Francisco—short, dark, a blue headband tied around his forehead—comes up the drive and asks if I need help.

He carries in a box of battered books, a suitcase, photo albums, my hippie bedspread, and some thin pillows. He smiles a half-smile that reveals bright, small teeth. He wears a blue headband, and his name is *Francisco*, not Frank. He smells of tobacco and something else I can't quite pinpoint: sage perhaps, the smell of the desert.

That half-smile reveals bright, small teeth. We're in redwood country, and the damp bark of the big trees rises all around us, canopies high overhead filled with birds: red-tailed hawks, osprey, flickers, and ravens. Yet, he smells of tobacco and the desert. The ravens call raucously, as if in warning, *caw! caw! caw!*

We're in redwood country, and the birds flock like omens: hawks, osprey, flickers, and ravens. I'll lie in my bed in that dark paneled room, aware of Francisco and his energy pulsing in a room on the other side of the house. The ravens wake me up with their *caw! caw! caw!* We'll play basketball together, and he'll dribble the ball by me, touch me just once on the hip with the back of his hand.

Later I'll lie in my bed in that dark paneled room, aware—so aware—of Francisco on the other side of the house. In my mouth, the taste of honey; in my knees, an ache. He touched me just once on the hip with the back of his hand. That's all it took to determine what happened next.

In my mouth the taste of honey. I baked loaves and loaves of bread for all the boys in that house, after the baby—the cluster of cells—was gone. That's all it takes sometimes: the crust of chewy bread and pats of butter to melt on the tongue. In the redwoods, he gave me the name Little Raven.

I baked loaves and loaves of bread for the boys in that house, after the baby was gone. I was twenty years old, barely an adult. On my tongue, the name Little Raven, a bird that seemed like a sentinel. The pain, like a penknife, stabbing again and again.

Aftershocks

In college, I once thought I caused an earthquake. Lying on my futon, on the floor of our old shared farmhouse in Arcata, after a fight with my boyfriend—and then the tremor. I recognized it instantly—*earthquake*—and in the next instant—*I'm sorry!* The apology blurted from my lips, and then the hushed wait for more, the hesitant cries, stirrings from others in the house. We stumbled out of our rooms, stood huddled on the front lawn. Stefan, studying to be a clown. The girl who taught tarot. The hippie guy with his golden retriever Jesse. The woman who suffered epileptic seizures that made her speak in tongues.

Her boyfriend, a coke dealer, would sometimes bring on the seizures on purpose, as if she were a parlor trick and, morbidly intrigued, we went along with it. We sat in a circle in the living room. I don't remember exactly the procedure—cocaine was involved, something to do with the lights—but what I do remember is the tender way he held her during it all. She was a skinny woman with glasses and wiry curls, wore dirndl skirts and ruffled blouses, the colors never quite matching. She was very quiet, hardly spoke; she kept her gaze on her boyfriend, a man with a sharp nose, sandy hair, a goatee on his narrow chin. He put a little mound of coke on the mirror for her to sniff, and then rocked her back and forth, singing a nonsense song. I remember a candle flickering as if in a séance.

Before long, her back started to arch, and he reached inside her mouth to unfurl her tongue. Her wrists curled, her arms shook, her legs trembled: a complete abandonment. She seized, and then went limp, her eyes open but dark as the night sky.

Here it comes, her boyfriend said, and she began speaking a language none of us knew but understood—the language of *occupation*, of *beyond*. Gurgling like a too-full stream, or a hosanna twisted in the throat. It lasted only a minute. She closed her eyes. He stroked her forehead, cradled her, cooed to her as if she were an infant.

Later that night—the earthquake. The moment the earth shook I thought it was my fault, felt sorry for everything: sorry for watching a woman's body in its most vulnerable moment; sorry for having a boyfriend who called upon spirits of his own, doused them in gin, spoke a different kind of tongue, his words cutting at every angle. The quake uttered, *What the hell are you doing? This is not the person you are meant to become.*

We stood on the lawn and waited for the aftershocks we knew would come. Jesse the retriever stood among us, ears erect, listening for whatever might be stalking us out there in the dark.

Scar

I have few regrets, but one is that I told my mother not to come. That time I had my second miscarriage: I was a junior in college, and I talked to her on the phone, said: *No, that would just make it worse.* I hung up and reached for the painkillers by my bed, the big ones I had to choke down.

I imagine now what would have happened if I'd said, *Yes, please come, I need you.* She would have boarded a plane, settling herself with her snacks and a favorite white sweater that she'd pull tight across her shoulders, afraid to be traveling alone. She would have arrived with cookies and gone out to buy mint chocolate-chip ice cream, my favorite, and she might even have spooned it into my mouth, the way she did when I was four years old and had my tonsils out. She'd have the same look in her eyes, that same laser focus finding me behind the bars of my crib.

I know now I would have been comforted and not ashamed. I would have learned how a mother will do anything to make sure her daughter is safe. But back then I was just a scared girl, cowering in my dark cave of a room, male roommates hovering out of sight. I talked to her on the phone, aloof and distant, while my fingers touched the incision that later would become a scar.

Giving Your Body to Science

You make such a fine specimen after all: reproductive organs deformed, something wrong in the blood, the cells. Cells that divided incorrectly, so you become a test case for interns who file into the room where you sit in your paper gown, feet in socks, smiling your crooked smile as they shuffle in nervously, not looking at you. You, a college girl who will be paid $30 for donating your living body to science, who will lie back and hook your feet in stirrups while nervous young hands practice putting in the speculum.

Speculum: such a strange word, like *speculation*, the nose of it nudging aside the most sensitive tissues so the curious may peer inside. They slip gloved fingers inside to diagnose the mystery: your strange cervix with its cockscomb hood, the errant cervical cells, a riddle for them to figure out on their own—you're a trick. Tricky to get the speculum in without hurting, so hurt you they do, yet they're the ones who wince, say *sorry, sorry, sorry* all in a rush as they put gloved hands inside, feel around, and one of them gets it, only one. One man who's proud of himself for divining what's wrong with you, even pats your knee as he says it—*DES Syndrome*—as if those words now form your name, as if he now owns you.

You smile again, say *Congratulations*—your pelvis aching as they file out. One of them—a young woman with straight black hair—says to you, surely against the rules: *Don't you feel weird doing this?* And then she's gone. Gone with the rest of them, and you wish you'd said something—something about the $30 and how it will buy groceries, something about helping womankind—but you wait silently in the empty room, staring at clear jars of cotton balls and Q-tips, the tongue depressors, the bandages, and metal cabinets shutting in all manner of secrets.

Operation

In 1970, my favorite game was Operation. I don't know what appealed to me so much—maybe the exposed interior of the man's body, gaping so that everything in him was revealed; or maybe it was the way you had to hold your breath as you reached inside him with your tweezers. You had to concentrate so hard that everything else dimmed into the background. You focused on a kidney or femur, the beat of your own blood now so insistent, making your hands tremble. You reached into the cavity and either emptied the man's body of his essential parts one by one, or you touched the boundary ever so slightly, but just enough to get shocked.

Sometimes I played the game by myself, just me and the man, his eviscerated body waiting for me to find his heart and remove it with delicate precision. He remained blank-faced as I reached inside him again and again. He would empty, and I filled him back up—this body continually resurrected.

The game broke after a while, and we lost all those little parts. But still, I sometimes made up my own game of Operation, lying on my bed in the afternoon—imagined my body opened up along the centerline, and within it all the parts waiting to be plucked: lung, heart, uterus, ovary. I drummed my fingers on my clavicle. Patted down my hipbones. Then grew very still, and waited for the buzz, wanting so much to be hollowed.

Sweat Lodge

We had a teacher in college who bustled into the classroom wearing a bear claw necklace and a turquoise belt buckle that flashed from beneath his belly. He smoked cigarettes in class, sometimes a pipe, saying, *Tobacco is my medicine.* We watched him carefully—both the white kids and the native kids—a little bit scared and a little bit awed. One white girl timidly raised her hand and asked if he could possibly, maybe, not smoke in class because the smell made her sick, and he said, *Well, I have to sit here and smell all you girls when you're menstruating,* so we shut up after that, just listened. Sometimes I skipped class when I was "on my moon," and Bobby approved of that, didn't mark it as an absence.

I often longed for the "moon huts" we read about in class, where women were sequestered at their time of the month. It didn't seem like a punishment to me but the most wonderful gift: to be absolved from all your day-to-day tasks while bleeding, to have a few days just to chat with your sisters and have food brought to you by an elder. It would be a little hiatus, an interlude, a haven from the world of men.

We read books like *Black Elk Speaks*, books with pictures of stoic Indians on the covers, books that made the white kids feel guilty and the native kids angry. The white kids got more and more depressed, looking at each other with despair, leaving class with downcast eyes, while my boyfriend Francisco and the other native students became a cabal of sorts, with our teacher and his wife. They started showing up in class wearing vests made of animal skins, big silver rings on their slender hands. They met off campus and took long treks into the woods along the shore. They smelled of tobacco and the tides.

Our teacher's wife was a shaman. When they drove us home one night, the headlights swept across the dark house, and ten cats shot out from underneath the floorboards, sprinting off in every direction. She shook her head and refused to come inside, said bad spirits inhabited that house. I believed in bad spirits, could feel them when I walked back to the dark cave of my room, where I put on the Grateful Dead loud enough to form a protective cocoon.

I thought maybe those spirits could be my own children: those babies I miscarried, and who hadn't quite left. Children who were really only nebulous ideas of children—a future I might have had as a married woman: two kids playing in the backyard, me watching them as I wiped my hands on a dish towel, thinking only of dinner and feeding them and waiting for my husband to come home. One boy and one girl, beautiful in the way all small children are terrifying and gorgeous, their eyes clear, alert, and watchful. We would eat dinner together and tell little family jokes, laughing at something ridiculous that no one else could ever understand.

I keep seeing the headlights sweep over the house, the cats streaking into the night. All I can do is keep getting out of that car over and over, walking toward the door with Francisco, fumbling for the lock, going inside and flipping on all the lights. I turned to him, wanting something, an answer perhaps, and he shrugged, the shrug that always disarmed me, made him look like a little boy gazing out from under his thick eyelashes. But just as quickly his eyes turned flinty and hard. He became a man again.

I would like to say I knew then it was time to leave, quickly as those cats, to make another spoke in the wheel and get somewhere far away, where the spirits couldn't follow. But everything, back then, seemed inexorable; I didn't know how to exorcise. So I went to the back of my house, toward my room, and Francisco followed like a shadow. Spirits move like shadows, or maybe the opposite of shadow—they are pure light, transparent. But they attach in the same way, move with you this way and that, can't be shaken off that easily.

But the spirits back then weren't all bad: some were kind, like the redwood, and some were authoritarian, like the red-tailed hawk. Some were simply playful, moving a toothbrush in the night or eating half an English muffin. I moved among them as carefully as possible. I knelt at their feet and asked, *What do you need from me? What do you want?* I listened to the silence. Made loaves and loaves of bread to feed them.

Years later I stoop to enter a sweat lodge in the California woods—stripped naked, carrying my wand of sage. Heat enters my pores, burns out any place a bad spirit might hide. Someone pours water over the rocks, and someone starts to cry, and we pray hard in our individual tongues. I pound myself with the fanned needles of a cedar branch; someone throws sage on the fire; we all pant like animals. Sweat pours down my belly, between my legs. I lie down flat on the earth, where I can get a little sip of air. I pray for that girl in a house surrounded by cats, stuck in the hub of an ugly mandala. I stumble outside and pour ice-cold water over my head. *What do you need from me? What do you want?* The manzanita waves. A nighthawk whooshes by. Albino deer tiptoe soundlessly along game trails in the dark.

Wild Mushrooms

We hunted wild mushrooms in the fields around Blue Lake, after the rains, the hills rising up fir-shouldered around us. The ocean shuddered four miles west, saying over and over again, *Hush*. Bent like old farmers, pant legs heavy with the damp, we scoured the ground, trying to find them: the 'shrooms that were camouflaged until you found just one fleshy brown cap, a fringed dunce's hat no bigger than your thumb, stalk slender and fragile as a reed. It led the way to others that suddenly appeared in your vision, as if they sprouted just that moment from the ground you'd already scanned a dozen times.

We grew quiet, focused. The mushrooms clustered in families around cow dung and shredded bark. We picked them carefully, placed them in our plastic bags, where they lay snugged against one another like pungent sardines. A VW van passed by on the highway and honked, and then another—friendly toots, as if to support our efforts.

It was serious business, these mushrooms we'd later sell on the square in Arcata, but for me I wanted only the hunt, a reason to be out in that field with this older man, an elusive man, one who also required the patience of a hunter. There in the quiet, both of us focused on the same goal, the pursuit of something small but powerful. Even in the ground, their brown bodies seemed to glisten with promise of alteration.

Later, I'd steep them in tea, sip them on the deck overlooking the valley, waiting for the moment my ordinary, earthbound self might vanish.

Headache

Once he had a bad headache. I don't know why I thought I could do anything about it, but I got up on the bed behind him, cupped my hands on his skull. He let me. He leaned back into me, all of him, giving up the rigid barrel chest, the tensed fists. I pressed my fingers through his hair, massaged the skin, felt the plates of bone in the skull, the way they barely connect, how everything's so tenuous. I closed my eyes. Felt a pain travel up my arm, sharp as an electrical shock. *Is it gone?* I asked.

I wrote a paper about it for my college class, typed it up on the old Remington I had in my room. I was out of black ink, so I typed it all in red. I said, *Maybe this means I'm a healer?* I wrote about his vision quest, the way he packed up his pipe in a little leather pouch. We sat on my bed and said goodbye as if he might not return.

I got an "A." The professor was kind. He said it wasn't a college paper, but he appreciated the details. He asked if I was all right. I said, *Sure, I'm all right.* He nodded and shut the door behind me when I left.

Groceries

In Page, Arizona, where Francisco and I moved after college, we always got the battered cart with its stuck wheel limping up and down the brightly-lit aisles full of canned vegetables, boxes of cereal, flour, milk. Milk and Kool-Aid and hominy, a little bit of tough pork—that's what we'd buy, though I'd thrown a fit over the cost of the Kool-Aid, calculated the price in my head, weighed the few bills in my pocket over the promise of sweetness to the water. The water at Wahweap Marina tasted metallic, and all he wanted was something to make it bearable, but I said it was a luxury we couldn't afford. (*Afford?* How did one calculate such things—I was only 23, had never run a household, knew nothing of budgets, remembered only my mother and her fan of coupons in hand at the checkout line, the careful way she counted up how much she had saved.)

Saving as much as I could of the $7 in my pocket, I said no to the Kool-Aid, and we fought right there in the soft drinks aisle— the Navajo shoppers knew to look away, familiar with fights held out in the open, hiding their disapproval of this white girl and Indian man duking it out over the Kool-Aid—while the white shoppers stared openly as they pushed their carts by us, until he finally threw ten packs of the powder into our cart—berry, lemon, lime, orange—and I slunk behind him to the checkout counter. At the counter, we placed on the conveyer belt our cans of hominy, our Wonder Bread, our little bit of pork, our white flour, and salt.

Salt at least made things taste better, and I watched it slide by, while I glanced at the magazines holstered in their racks, then we bagged everything up, took the lone sack back to our trailer, where I doled out salt into the *posole*, measured with the cup of my palm, the skin there red and cracked from the cold.

Beloved

"And what did you want?
To call myself beloved, to feel myself
beloved on the earth."
—Raymond Carver

O n Lake Powell, the silence grows so deep it pulses against your ears, and the water lapping on the shore is the very definition of cold comfort. You sit alone, rocking in the motorboat, your boom box tinnily playing Fleetwood Mac; it's the only thing here that's truly yours, while you watch the dock, waiting for him to emerge from the store. This store carries bait, motor oil, potato chips, Fritos, Styrofoam coolers, and drinks, lots of drinks: water and Pepsi and Gatorade and beer.

Beer, you know, is what he'll emerge with, a case of something cheap, and he'll carry it with a swagger: hiding it and flaunting it at once. Your neck prickles as you wait, the boat rocking, the water slapping the sides of the deck, Stevie Nicks singing of leather and lace, her voice barely denting the silence of the high desert— absorbed by the high red rocks, the unreal blue water, and the drowned trees beneath the surface.

This cool air in the desert, over the water: it's a land of contradiction, the light bright and subdued at once. You can motor along the wide expanse of the lake, find a small canyon to enter and look for the hanging gardens: plants growing high above the water line, gaining foothold and flourishing on bare rock, while beneath you—far beneath—a ghost garden mirrors the one above.

You thought you were going to Rainbow Bridge, where all the tourists go, that huge arch spanning the sky. A place, they say, that is full of spirits, and the natives here say it is a bridge to the after-life—or used to be anyway, before all the tourists came, before all the boats broke the silence and everyone was so eager to set foot on sacred soil.

But it turns out you're not going to Rainbow Bridge after all; he shoves the beer into the boat's stern, doesn't look at you, moves quickly to untie the boat and steer you out in the opposite direc-tion: away from the shoreline, with its many attractions, and into the flat wide expanse of water unbounded by anything—water that looks blue from a distance, but close up becomes black.

You know you shouldn't say anything, should just sit back and admire the stark beauty all around you—the smooth granite of Gunsight Butte, the water snaking its way through the wide river canyon—but you get out into open water, and he cuts the engine, and he cracks the first one open, the pull tab creaking loudly against your ears. He drinks long and hard, the way men do who are this kind of thirsty.

Your hands grip the gunwales, and you can't help it: you say, *I thought you weren't going to drink*, but your voice is insubstantial, weak as Stevie Nicks who sings from far inside the boom box. He throws the empty can overboard, and you watch it bobbing, *Budweiser* in blood-red letters curling against the black. And you see now you're really far from shore, and you're starting to burn in that exposed area of your neck, that little strip your shirt fails to cover.

He says nothing, but leans toward you, another beer in hand. He picks up the boom box by its handle and looks at it appraisingly. Stevie Nicks keeps singing as it sways in his hand. You spent more money than you had on that tape player, and it traveled with you from California to Arizona, keeping you company on all those nights alone. Your stash of cassettes is well-worn—full of hand-lettered liner notes that have faded to barely distinguishable words. You have lots of bootleg Grateful Dead tapes that you listen to over and over, remembering when you could dance with abandon. Many of the tapes have broken, but you keep them anyway, as reminders.

I could throw this thing in the lake right now, he says, his voice soft, but his eyes hard. He holds it a few moments longer, then drops it on the seat, and the music clatters to a halt. Stevie Nicks shuts up, the way you should have done, should have just kept quiet. You imagine you and Stevie are in this boat together, huddled against one another, groping for each other's hands.

Or I could throw you *overboard*, he says, not really to you, but to himself. A threat, but not a threat, just a statement of fact.

He puts his free hand back on the rudder, drinks his beer while turning toward a side canyon, toward a cove with a beach of white sand. A place that in any other time, with any other person, would be a romantic picnic spot—the water lapping, the rock sheltering— and you putter in, anchor the boat, slosh your way toward shore. He has cans of beer stuffed in every pocket. You don't know what will happen next.

You're not lost: that will happen later, when he begins walking up a trail to the mesa, and you'll follow because what else is there to do? You'll climb in the hot sun (no cool air now, no breeze, no comfort) until you reach the top, where you'll be able to see now— in a way you never could from below, when you're immersed in it—the expanse of this land, cracked and broken. No straight line between here and there, between past and future; instead, many small rifts open between where you stand now and where you are trying to go.

Bright Angel

I once hitchhiked alone across the Arizona desert to the Grand Canyon. Once there, I lightened my backpack of everything non-essential. I hiked down the Bright Angel trail, camped on the Colorado, and then trudged back up to the rim. I had a little backpacking tent that weighed only two pounds. I had a tin cup that seemed to weigh nothing at all, with my "Indian name," Little Raven, scrawled on the bottom with magic marker. I wore a dirty bandana on my head.

The water got to you; you had to carry enough to see you through. Halfway to the top, I set up my tent in the Garden of the Gods, my water supply dwindling, and gazed out into the abyss. More intrepid backpackers hiked past me, intent on making it up top in a day. I felt no hurry to return.

The only way to get there was by sticking out my thumb. Something must have kicked in for me, a guardian angel perhaps. Not that I really believed in a guardian angel. Well, actually, I did believe, fervently, even when the angel had been on furlough a long while. I did stupid things, but something kept me safe. Safe enough to see what would happen next.

I thought of the buddy system we'd had in school: one kid assigned to be your buddy as you made the dangerous excursion across the street, or across town, holding her sweaty hand in your sweaty hand, looking both ways. You sat next to each other on the school bus, then watched for the tip of her red cap or the sheen of her blond hair in the crowded planetarium. Sometimes you got a buddy who wanted to be your buddy, and sometimes you got someone dismayed to be your buddy, her face crestfallen, but no matter what, you took your job seriously, made sure she was on the bus, raised your hand with solemn authority when the teacher asked, *Okay, you have your buddy?* And then the bus could roll away, full—no one lost, no one hurt, no one left behind.

The bus smelled of roast-beef sandwiches and Sprite and bubble gum. You looked out the window, your buddy at your side, and thought about the planetarium, the way all the kids swarmed into their seats and then hushed as the lights went down and the stars emerged above you, first one, then two and three, then billions, and then—gasp!—a shooting star and a collective *Oh!* lifting us from our seats. The announcer's deep voice intoned the mysteries of outer space, telling us how unseen forces—gravity, orbital pull, magnetism—keep the heavenly bodies in place. A single star might have been bright enough to grab our attention, but more often the constellations drew us helplessly into their violent stories—each star a relative to another one far away.

The bus rolled away, your head full of stars, or perhaps it was the tar pits at the L.A. County Museum of Art and the pictures of mammoths, a pair of them struggling to lift their giant hairy legs out of the muck, their massive trunks trumpeting a plea for help. Or maybe it was the production of Hansel and Gretel on the stage at the L.A. Forum, the brother and sister so tiny on the stage far below as they dodged danger together, found their way out from under the witch's grasp.

Your buddy sat beside you, smelling of peanut butter. Everyone grew quiet as the unfamiliar streets gradually morphed into the familiar, and you recognized the farthest reaches of your territory;

you trundled by Hughes shopping center and Love's Barbecue and Farrell's ice cream parlor, and then you grew older and a different bus pulled up to the gates of the junior high, then the high school, and at some point they decided you were too old to have a buddy, so you had to disembark alone.

Quite a Storm

Those storms in the desert, you can see them coming from a long way off: dark clouds roiling, wind picking up, jagged bolts of lightning flashing and touching ground, each one quick and sharp. You listen for the thunder rolling up behind, wait for the moment when everything will be synchronized— and then you know you're in it, in the center, trees bending and shaking, something rattling the roof, lightning and thunder now one animal trying to get in. The only thing between you and the storm is the sliding glass door, and you see the jackrabbits going for cover.

You know the power will go out, and you'll have to find the flashlight and batteries, candles and matches; you'll have to eat all the food in the fridge before it goes bad, and you'll still have to get up at 4 a.m. and drive to work. You'll dash from the truck into the rain and wind, knock frantically at the locked glass door for the baker to let you in—the baker who, weeks earlier, had looked you up and down, and said: *Why does a college girl like you want a job like this?* You'd had no answer for that question, but you still got the job because you were white and sober and scared.

So now you run inside, shake off the rain, put on the big white apron, and start pressing fresh donuts into frosting, sprinkling them with chocolate jimmies and coconut, scooping out the powdered sugar and glaze.

You clean the glass cases, squeaking your rag over the slanted panes to get out every last smudge, then slide the trays of perfect donuts inside, listening to country music or Fleetwood Mac, the baker grunting softly in back, hazy in a cloud of flour. You set up the big coffeepot, and you unlock the door, and you wait behind the counter, your wet hair now dry and dusted with sugar, a smile on your face as you pick up the donuts with wax paper, hand them to the waiting men, all of them saying, *Quite a storm last night*, and you echo back, *Quite a storm*, the smile careful on your face, and you look out the windows to see light reflecting from the puddles on the street. Your mouth tastes like sugar gone sour, and you keep stooping to pick out the donuts the men request, sliding them into bags or boxes or just on a napkin, the heft of them between your fingers a comfort, and a comfort, too, the way your body has learned how to move so quickly, to get what it needs, to bend.

Box Canyon

Sometimes there's no road at all—just a game trail through the desert, a faint track that leads past piñon pine and prickly pear, zigzagging across the rust-colored dirt, always heading toward water, perhaps just an underground spring emerging as a damp trickle under a green bush. You sniff it out, the sky wide overhead, a breeze you can't feel moving the spare branches against the canyon walls. You keep following it until you come to a dead end: the box canyon, a place where the Indians used to drive wild horses, knowing there'd be no way out, the wild ones snorting and snuffling against the cliff, while the tamed horses grew inflamed with the hunt, sweat on their flanks, high-stepping sideways. The Indians threw their lassos, caught the horses by their necks, coaxed them out of the canyon and into the fold, thundering out of the desert. Sometimes you think you still see wild horses on the ridge: their small backs, their heads turning to watch you as you make your way along the watershed. You're watched, too, by coyote and rattlesnake, jackrabbit and scorpion, as you zigzag across the desert, the vultures overhead, but you make your way out, you find the familiar stones, the ones that can lead you home.

Altered Fruit

The summer I left him, I worked in California as a cook for a youth camp ten miles down a dirt road out of Willits. I applied for the job by making soup. It must have been satisfactory—something hearty, like split pea or chili—because they gave me the job. I wouldn't start for another week, so I camped by myself on a knoll above the farm, because I had nowhere else to go.

During that week alone, I soaked dried apricots and figs in warm water, ate them with almonds and pecans. I was thin for a cook. Every day I soaked my ration of fruit in warm water, waiting patiently for the rehydration, the plumping of the flesh—apricots and peaches and pears. Of course this fruit was nothing like the original—the flesh too sweet, like candy—but it tasted ambrosial. I rationed out the nuts to go with it, ate slowly, slowly, like someone trapped, like a woman who doesn't know when she will be rescued. I sat in that tent and wrote letters and watched the turkey vultures in their rickety orbits over the hills.

Hours in silence: reading my book in the tent, the pages swollen and damp. I peeked out the canvas door and watched the vultures flap their enormous wings—slowly, slowly—as they hopped drunkenly from limb to limb, five of them clotting in the branches of an oak. Something must have died there, on the ground, and they waddled forward to pick at the carcass. I looked away, thought of the desert, the small raptors swooping across a canyon. The ravens cawing in circles, the dry ground bristling with thorns.

I walked in the rain, went back inside, listened to the rain, and ate my altered fruit slowly, slowly, until it was time to go back down the mountain and start my life over.

I came down from the mountain, every part of me moist, my skin flushed and translucent. They had me sleep in a little cabin by the river. I read cookbooks at night, memorizing the recipes, instructions floating through my mind like mantras: *measure, warm, simmer, stir.* I improvised soups from fresh zucchini, potatoes, green beans. I sent children to tear corn off the stalk minutes before dinner, peered out the screened window to see them running with the cobs back to the kitchen, shrieking, racing to husk them before sugar turned to starch.

One girl picked raspberries all day long, spoke to no one, couldn't look me in the eye as she handed me the brimming bowls. The children and I baked bread: sourdough and whole wheat and rye. We made hamburger buns and cinnamon rolls. We cranked out the world's longest noodle, the campers holding it aloft like a sacred thing, laughing as they tumbled with it down the back steps.

We drank spring water from tin cups etched with animal names. Mine said, *Black-tailed Doe.* An ordinary animal, beautiful but wary, her small ears twitching in the dusk.

There's a picture of me from that summer—with my hair clipped back, an apron across my skirt, a mysterious smile on my face as I make a huge pan of cinnamon rolls with the children. My gaze aims at the butcher block and the dough, a small ball of it pinched between my fingers. And there's another picture of me standing in a river, the Mendocino hills in the backdrop, my pants rolled up to the knee, jeans on over my bathing suit—and my gaze is exactly the same: tilted downward, that mysterious smile, as if I can't bear to look directly at anyone, as if I'm looking only at myself.

I'm slender in this photo, and my cheekbones are high, my arms smooth and thin, my feet underwater. I know how cold that water must have been against the heat of a California summer. The children must have been cavorting in the shallows, and I stood apart, as I always did, just watching.

Years later, I'll come across the photo as I'm cleaning a closet and I'll hardly be able to fathom that girl now, thirty years later, another lifetime passed since the moment I stood in a river, thinking of . . . what? Perhaps gratitude for the hills and the river and the farm and the children and the food, but wondering about my next step: if I should go deeper into that river and submerge, perhaps emerge a different person altogether. I believed in baptism. I believed in immersion.

Perhaps that's why I'd done my enforced, ascetic diet in the tent on those hills in the background, friendly mountains that oversaw my fast. I submerged into the darkest parts of myself before emerging to cook on this family farm—where I would smile my mysterious smile and sit on picnic tables and sing "Kumbaya." In this song, someone's always crying, someone's always laughing, someone's always singing, and everyone is praying for release. In those hills, I could feel myself shriveling like a raisin, not dry but more concentrated, the sweetest part of me gathering. And the guitarist closed his eyes, and the children swayed as they sang; the vultures kept circling, and we all lifted our faces toward the sky.

Understand

In Alaska, you understand how light is now a substance of its own making—tactile, with particles and waves and something else. You understand how light finds the least pinhole and expands. Now you know why those who got lost got lost. You feel the lure of those mountains—or not the mountains but the rifts between them. You understand the need to fill rifts. To get closer.

Alaska. So far from the deserts of Arizona, from your home suburb of L.A. The word opens in your mouth. *Alaska!* This word contains its own exclamation. In Aleut, *Alaska* means, "the object toward which the action of the sea is directed." You understand the action of the sea. You feel the sea's attention on you, a woman who won't look away. You say, *Okay.* You say, *Ah.* You say, in a mumble, at 2 a.m., *Enough already with the light.*

You find yourself on the beach at midnight. How did you get here? Understand that time is no longer time in Alaska. Understand that sleep is merely a concept—your blood too jittery with light. It has discarded the map. It goes this way and that, filling rifts that never knew how to fill. Rifts that never know—only open incrementally, glaciers receding to leave rubble.

You thought the word *understand* meant to "stand under." And you stand underneath them: these mountains, this sky full of its eagles, this sea full of otter and puffin. But, no—to understand is to "stand in the midst of." It means, "between." There is no hierarchy, no *above* or *below*. There is only *among*. It means, "to be close to." It means, "put together."

So, you piece yourself together. You grow close, you are *among*—nearsighted and farsighted at once, with your tiny self waving in between. Walk a beach at midnight and see twilight oozing through the canyons on the far shore. Stare at the smooth rocks at your feet, but do not stoop to pick them up, do not even think of skipping.

PART III

Regeneration

"It looks like a ghost heart. And it feels a little like Jello."
—Doris Taylor, bioengineer

I

On the radio show *Speaking of Faith*, researcher Doris Taylor is telling us how to build a new heart. They take a cadaver heart, she says, wash away all the dead cells with shampoo until only a "ghost heart" remains. This ghost heart will provide the scaffold for stem cells that will create the new heart on their own.

I look at pictures of the ghost heart on the website: it looks a little bit like halibut: white-fleshed, resilient, translucent. It's almost all water, with just enough structure to hold it in the shape of a heart. She will implant a stem cell on this medium and wait for it to start beating. The cells know what to do—she just has to create the environment for everything to happen at once.

We're regenerating the heart on many different levels, she says. *Physically, emotionally, spiritually. If you put a new heart back in the same environment, it's going to get damaged again.*

II

In her installation, *The Sound of Cells Dividing*, Geraldine Ondrizek invites us into small, cellular rooms made of translucent paper, where we're allowed an auditory glimpse of what the body sounds like. Our bodies emit music, something mathematicians have known all along. The artist has recorded the way a needle can play our cells like a phonograph, the pitches of music harmonizing, disharmonizing. We sit inside one paper fort, and then another, to listen, entranced.

In another room of the gallery, Ondrizek has embroidered the DNA of her dead son on the binder of the Torah. She tattooed his genetic makeup on the cloth. His body has evaporated, gone, but a ghost body remains.

As I look, the dead son's chromosomes morph into the shape of a tree of life. The background: a flurry of stains, amniotic, smudged fluids of birth. She has stitched a recording, a threaded calligraphy. I imagine her at this work, bent over the needle and thread for years, toiling to inscribe her son on the surface of the world.

III

My friend tells me it's called *neurogenesis*.

It's because you're actually creating new pathways in the brain. Not a new brain exactly, but new ways for the brain to fire, he tells me.

We're in my kitchen, just the two of us, while the rest of my guests sit in the living room, talking loudly, laughing. The lights of the menorah candles we've just lit burn merrily away. Two organic chickens roast in the oven, stuffed with apples and onion. I've laden a tray with *latkes*. I've made a honey-curry braided bread studded with slivers of golden almonds, and I have a white platter of raspberry-chocolate *macarons* waiting on the sideboard. The kitchen smells of rosemary and cumin, paprika, fried potatoes. We will eat around my coffee table, and afterward play a game of Taboo that will have us laughing so hard we'll be gasping for breath.

Neurogenesis. A new brain. A synaptic beginning. I let the dog outside and turn to my friend, my good friend for years now. He has had his own struggles with the brain. I turned fifty this year and have just started taking Celexa, an antidepressant that comes in the smallest pill imaginable.

I never thought I would take it: I wanted my brain to be *my* brain, the brain I always knew, no matter how often and how regularly it turned against me. I took Prozac for two days fifteen years ago, and I ended up crouched in a corner with my head in my hands, calling the psychiatrist and asking for an antidote. *There is no antidote*, she said impatiently. *Just wait for the side effects to pass.*

So I had stubbornly refused to even consider medications for these many years. Besides, I thought, wasn't it normal to feel the way I felt? Wasn't it an ordinary condition: to be slightly blue most of the time, to feel terrible about yourself even when all evidence points to the contrary? Don't we all stare out the window, waiting for something to change?

IV

February, 1963: I'm four years old and waiting for my mother to come home. I'm staring out the kitchen window; she's been gone two days, and I know something's up, something big. I've got a fat crayon clutched in my fist. My mother's in the hospital, giving birth to my baby brother, though I don't really understand what that means.

I would like to remember my mother's pregnant belly. I would like to remember touching that rounded, taut stomach, perhaps placing my lips against the belly button and kissing my nascent brother through this dome of flesh. I would like to imagine the complex smell of this belly—layered with sweat and baby powder, and smooth against my own baby cheeks—and my brother kicking me through the skin, me babbling his name over and over so he would know me when he arrived.

But I don't remember any of this. Instead I see myself alone at a kitchen table, writing with a big blue crayon a "welcome home" card, or a "happy birthday" card for this new child that has been living inside my mother, generating cell by cell, alive and not yet alive. I want to touch him. I want to be touched by this ghost creature who's about to arrive.

A neighbor has been taking care of my older brother and me, and she slapped me when I cried for my mother too long. She apologized immediately, made me cinnamon toast, but her hand has left its mark. It has told me I'm not strong enough to be in this world alone.

I want my mother returned to me in her normal pressed slacks, her cotton sweater, and her lipstick so perfectly applied with a brush. I hear a car turn onto the cul-de-sac, see the station wagon making its careful glide up Amestoy Avenue. I can see through the passenger window the vague shape of my mother, holding a bundle in her arms. Something flutters up in me: love, long-ing, excitement, anger, fear—all of them, all at once. I wait at the window to see what will happen next. I touch my own belly, the crayon still in my hand, and leave a mark there that will take forever to wash out.

V

I wonder if they'll be able to rebuild a brain next. To wash away the one you have: all those cells with their unhelpful memories, those flawed synapses, down the drain. You'd be left with a "ghost brain"—pale, and bland as Jello.

VI

I would like to put my ear up against the walls of my own cells. I would like to listen to what my cells have to say. You have to stay in Geraldine Ondrizek's paper cells a long time to get it: to hear the voices of family in the background, the chanting of monks from their monastic cells, and then—always, behind it all—a vast silence.

I wonder if it's really the silence I've been after all this time: the amniotic pause of the womb, the whispered hush of paper, the space where we can all be reborn.

Gizzards

"... *cheer up, cheer up, cheer up ...*"
— Kelli Russell Agodon

That voice in my head: maybe not my own, but the mutter of my grandmother, or her mother, as they wiped down counters, dressed their children, cut up chickens one by one— *cheer up, cheer up, cheer up.*

Cheer up, the chop of the cleaver. *Cheer up*, clean break of a thigh. *Cheer up*, the gizzards, the heart, a liver glistening in hand. I wonder: can they pause, stunned to silence by viscera? Evidence of interiority, shellacked by what contains them. They must have felt—how else to put it?—a visceral tug: reminder of one's own glutinous heart, and the liver so mysterious, filtering, always filtering, the bladder secreting gall—organ meat, so unlike exterior flesh.

More tender? More alive, once exposed on a grandmother's palm. *Cheer up, cheer up, cheer up*, she hums and fries cubes of liver with circles of onion, cracks the shells of hard-boiled eggs, renders *schmaltz* from chicken fat, chops them all together in the shallow wooden bowl, rocking with the rounded chopper, twin blades curved like scythes, wood handle worn smooth.

Cheer up, cheer up, cheer up: a mantra to work by. *Chop it up chop it up chop it up*, until everything mingles in one lovely mound. Apron dotted with blood, hands plump and clean, she stops a moment in her rocking and listens. Listens for grandchildren who clamor for chopped liver on thick slices of challah. Who cling in more ways than one. She listens for all those children who need cheering up, even those yet to be born.

36 Holes

". . . as if by emptying it could be filled,
or filled, emptied . . ."
—Catherine Barnett

1. They trundle an excavator in through the side yard, tear
   the old stump of the Rainier cherry from its useless roots. It
   must be loud, messy, almost violent: this unearthing, these
   men digging a hole in my backyard. They are doing all this
   work while I'm gone, so I don't need to witness the upheaval.
   It must scare the cat; I know I'll find her as a haggard lump
   under the covers when I get home. The men keep digging
   and digging, looking for good earth on which to build.

2. And so it begins, as most things do—with a hole.

3. For over two months, thirty-three Chilean miners have
   been trapped underground in a mine collapse. It's a story
   that seems impossible in its dimensions: all these men sur-
   viving the collapse in the first place, then being found, a
   small borehole drilled a half mile to make contact. The
   first missive: "We're all alive." The rescuers lowered down
   supplies—protein drinks, aspirin—and told them to wait,
   to not give up hope. They brought NASA on board to help

the men deal with confinement. They had counselors speaking down into the hole to help the men with anxiety and depression. The relatives kept watch in Camp Hope. We kept watch for a little while, waiting to see what would happen next. Then most of us forgot all about them.

4. When I was nineteen years old, a fertilized egg made a microscopic hole in my fallopian tube. When I was twenty, the other tube, not to be outdone, copied the first one. Another hole; another atomic explosion. I felt the first one as it occurred, a kind of ripping. The second time, I'd become wise to their shenanigans, knew the little tug from inside, got onto the exam table so the doctors could peer inside my most hidden tissues. The ultrasound tech was not sympathetic. She kept her face closed as she rubbed the ice-cold wand on my bloated belly, pushed into my full bladder. I don't remember the doctor arriving, don't remember the sentence he gave. I only remember the shivering.

5. My dog, when I give her a rawhide bone, immediately runs with it to the bedroom, where she tries to dig a hole in the carpet. My home is riddled with imaginary holes.

6. When I was a kid, I used to play in a hole in our backyard. Well, not really a hole, more of a wide depression that filled with water when it rained. My father, so fastidious about his lawn, could never quite get this depression under control, so every time it rained in L.A. (almost monsoons—they made mudslides out of the rich neighborhoods on the coast), we got a lake in our backyard. I splashed in it by myself, made up stories of treacherous, impossible water crossings. When

the rain stopped and the sun came out, the water dried up quickly and you could hardly tell there'd been a hole at all.

7. Sometimes depression feels like a hole you fall into—that's how many people describe it. You're walking along, and then *whoops*, in you go, tumbling down and down and down. You can smell the dirt. You get jabbed by the rough ends of roots, the hard nubs of rock. It's dark in a hole, depending on its depth. Some holes are shallow and some are deep. All of them require the knowledge that you're in a hole in the first place, in order to start climbing out.

8. And now, in the middle of our night, the thirty-three miners ascend through a long hole, one by one in a capsule built just large enough for a single man, arms wrapped around his chest, like a sarcophagus. The trip takes twenty minutes. One miner describes it as being *like a cruise*. One miner drops to his knees in prayer the minute he emerges. One miner runs through the crowd trailing the Chilean flag, leads them all in a raucous anthem. The first miner greets his four-year-old son who cries and cries and cries. All the miners are hugged, hard. Wives, mothers, fathers, sons, daughters, girlfriends, and the country's President hug them. We keep watching, anxious to see again and again that first poke of the capsule through the rim, that sign of life, the earth disgorging its hostages. They all wear sunglasses during this rescue, even at night, because it can hurt the eyes to come back into the world.

9. In the hole in my lawn they've found an old garbage pit. This new hole was once a hole already, used by families for

decades to get rid of things they didn't want. I don't know what's in this garbage pit because I'm gone, but they do tell me, indirectly, that this will cost me. They have to dig down deeper than they thought, because garbage makes for insecure footings. You can't build on top of garbage, they explain.

10. That's the thing about holes. They're just begging to be filled.

11. There is some debate about which hole in the earth is the largest. Some say in Mirny, Eastern Siberia, Russia. Some say in Bingham Canyon, Utah. Some say a diamond mine in South Africa. The more it gets discussed, the more holes there turn out to be, and hole aficionados become incensed about the accuracy of data, the skewing of statistics. Metrics vs. feet vs. altitude vs. surface width, etc., etc. Almost all these holes were created to extract something: diamonds, copper, coal. At least one was dug to explore the properties of the earth's crust. The hole in Siberia was dug by hand, hours and years and decades of moving dirt. They do not want to fill in these holes. A filled hole, in this case, would defeat the purpose.

12. A donut is defined by its hole. A donut without a hole is a donut hole. But a donut hole is not the hole gouged out from a donut; it is a donut of its own making.

13. When I was twelve my dentist pulled out nearly every tooth in my head; well, that's how my mother put it. I think it was nine teeth, maybe more, I can't remember. Baby teeth I hadn't lost yet, and some adult teeth that tried to muscle

their way into places they could never fit. I have a small mouth, apparently, and big teeth: the perfect combination for the orthodontist's coffers. They gave me a light anesthesia for the oral surgery, light enough so I remained conscious, but deep enough so I wouldn't feel any pain. I saw several heads leaning over me, obscured by bright lights. At one point I heard someone say, *The teeth are flying!* And I imagined them yanking all my teeth out with glee: white teeth clattering against the walls, dropping to the floor like hard snow. Afterward they gave me all my teeth in a plastic cup: some were still bloody, with yellow roots; some were small perfect squares, with each ridge of molar perfectly defined. I ran my tongue over the holes in my gums, tasted blood and spit, felt the ache rise as the anesthesia receded. For days afterward my mother fed me milk shakes, soups, soft bread. I felt my gums swell and contract, felt the holes readjust themselves to the shape of my gums.

14. I tune into the live video feed just as they crank the thirteenth miner out of the ground—a twenty-seven-year-old man whose mother waits on the sidelines as her boy travels through the earth's crust. She rubs her hands together, over and over. It feels as though we could just as easily be watching a journey the other way, a re-entry from the cosmos in a rocket ship. The capsule looks like a rocket, and it fits just barely through the passage as it aims its way toward light. Twenty-one inches wide: the miners, in their last days underground, had to be monitored to make sure they would fit. By now, they've been eating well: cylinder-shaped *empanadas* and other delicacies throughout their ordeal. There are rumors of a book deal, a movie treatment. The

rescuers have been at it several hours during the night—as soon as one miner arrives they ready the empty capsule for the next descent. The capsule—so shiny and new, painted in the colors of the Chilean flag—already looks worn and battered from its travels.

15. There are holes in my memory now. Holes that never used to be there. I'm not talking full-fledged amnesia, though that condition fascinated me as a child: to imagine a woman walking around without any recollection of who she is, piecing it together through ID cards, stories, looking intently into the eyes of companions who try to reconstruct life, and a memory, for them. I pictured myself wandering a lonely street, a body without a brain, the brain now blank, the brain its own messy and subterranean hole. I didn't admit it at the time, but I kind of loved the silly movie *50 First Dates*; in it a woman wakes up each morning with her short-term memory gone. Her husband has to recreate for her her life, bit by bit. He leaves her notes, they make a video. Eventually she's able to progress, to have a child, a family: each day swimming out of that hole like a diver with her finds.

16. *Into Perfect Spheres Such Holes Are Pierced.* Catherine Barnett wrote this book of poems after her two young nieces were killed in a commercial plane crash. Alaska Airlines Flight 411. It's a plane crash all of us in the Northwest vaguely remember, somewhere in the back of our minds—no survivors, all of them coming home to Seattle. And just ordinary people, like us. Barnett and her sister—the girls' mother—will never be able to forget. Will not want to forget. Will imagine it over and over, the girls suddenly let loose into the sky. In

this case, rescue is impossible. They will never be returned. Each word in that title stabs, even the word *perfect*. Each word, its own precise little hole.

17. The holes in me are not perfect. A little ragged around the edges. A little hard to trace.

18. Those two fallopian tubes have mended their holes, but are no longer intact. That means every month an egg pierces the membrane of my ovary and travels its jolly way down that fleshy tube, singing its ovulation song, primping for its encounter with the man of her dreams. And then *wham*: that wall of scar tissue says, *No dice.* She flattens, slides to the floor with a splat.

19. My neighbor's cat died when it was shot with a BB gun. Two microscopic holes, almost invisible, in her hip. *Who is killing our cats?* Michele asked. I kept my cat indoors for a while, but soon she was out again, looking for trouble.

20. As a kid I wanted to be swallowed by quicksand. I wondered what it must be like to sink in like that, to feel the pull of the earth drawing you deeper toward the center. To watch the world's surface disappear, bit by bit: goodbye first to the trees' tops, then the trunks, then you're swimming among the roots. Because that's what it comes down to, right? The root.

21. They keep the camera focused on the mother, who wears sunglasses so you can't see her eyes, but she keeps wiping away tears with her index finger. Her hard hat falls off every time someone comes over to give her a hug. They've been

waiting a long time for this, all the relatives, waiting for their sons, husbands, fathers to come back. They must have lain on the ground, felt the earth with their whole bellies, turned their cheeks to hear whatever they could. To say, *I love you.* To say, *Be strong.* Hoping a voice doesn't have to be just a voice, but can be a whole person traveling through layers of rock, veins of copper, striations of mud. We're all crying now: thousands of us sobbing as we bear witness to the impossible.

22. Holes for the light fixtures, holes for the outlets, holes for the windows, the doors. It seems impossible that the walls could ever become solid, something to keep you safe.

23. When the men are done with all their holes, I stand out on my new deck, and I can see molehills on my lawn. They spring up every morning, in different places, though I have yet to see a mole, yet to have my cat bring home a mole, and yet to see an actual mole *hole*. The phrase "holy moley," they say, comes from the plant used by the Greek gods to turn a man who had been turned into a pig back into a man. Mortals can't pick this plant, or even distinguish its white flower, its black stem. But maybe moles can. Moles, as they tunnel underground, searching among the roots.

24. I thought there was a connection between *hole* and *holy*. Though it turns out *holy* is more related to *whole*, with a *w*. But oh, how I want that false correlation!

25. The way holiness seems shot through with holes, like lace.

26. Sometimes I can still feel my ovaries churning out those tired eggs, with their frowny faces and tired passage to nowhere. *Can we just stop this now?* I imagine them saying, dragging their feet as they're shoved out the door. A different kind of digging a hole and filling it in again, pointlessly, over and over.

27. Or maybe it's a phantom pain. The kind that remains even when the source of pain is gone. This is a different kind of hole, the kind you can't fill because it doesn't really exist.

28. When I woke from my colonoscopy, I opened my eyes and saw my friend Nancy there at the bedside. I said, *Hello.* She said, *Hello.* Later, she told me that I had talked to the doctor for ten minutes before I woke again. *Really?* I asked. I searched my mind and could not pull up one shred of that conversation. It bothered me for days, bothers me still: these ten minutes I've lost forever. But something broke its way through the forgetting drug. That night, I dreamed a sharp pain in my abdomen, something snipping away there in the dark.

29. I once knew a painter who painted only the spaces in-between, ethereal washes of aqua blues and greens, the faintest yellows. There was depth to them, something that drew you in. I could stare at her paintings for a long time and feel for a little while what it's like to exist in a hole with no edges, no boundaries, no circumference. A hole without its rim—is it still a hole? Or something else?

30. A-hole. Pie-hole. As in, *Shut your pie-hole.* There's something disparaging about the word hole. You say it enough, and

you begin to feel angry. *Hole, hole, hole*, you mutter like a madman, talking to yourself.

31. Jigsaws, I hadn't realized, are really a memory game; you keep scanning the pieces, trying to match those pieces to the holes you've memorized, looking for bits of color that give you clues. I can hardly stand it when I've got a perfect hole in the middle of a cluster of pieces I've fitted together so triumphantly, and there it is: one perfectly outlined piece, announcing its singular shape, giving hints as to the exact color it needs, and *I can't find it.* I scan the unhooked pieces over and over, carefully separate them, and still it's gone. Always I think it's gone forever, that even though this is a *brand new* puzzle, there must be something missing. But my friend Chris is unflappable. He sits on the other side of the table, moving pieces around with a placid confidence, his glasses pushed up cock-eyed on his forehead. *They always turn up*, he says, without veering his glance away from the puzzle. *Just when you think it's impossible.*

32. So many things turn up just when you think it's impossible.

33. Holey things: Lace, a vulnerable fabric, so easily torn. The tattered wing of a dragonfly. A snag in the forest, shot through with the tappings of a woodpecker—that Morse code in the woods. Morse code itself, meaning made only through the spaces between each dot.

34. It's too facile to call it a rebirth, too parallel in its imagery— the boy, now a man, delivered through this long passage into the light. All the miners look remarkably clean and

healthy, but they must be ragged inside, must be on the verge of exhaustion. I'm sure the miner smells pungent, steeped in his two-month ordeal. His mother must inhale that scent greedily, her boy, her boy. The triage guys take him from her, lay him on a gurney, cover him with a blanket. Even though he still wears the sunglasses to protect his eyes, you can tell those eyes are closing. You can see his body surrender immediately to the soft pillow, the suspension of the gurney. His mother leans over him one more time, kisses him, feels his cheeks the way a mother will do. He turns his head slightly, mouths something softly that only she can hear, only she can understand.

35. John Cage lives in the spaces in-between. In his music, he shows us what resides in those spaces where nothing exists, but where everything belongs. He, in essence, creates a hole, a hollow place that holds anything we want to put inside.

36. All the miners had jobs to do, down there in the rescue chamber. They had to keep building walls, adding reinforcements. They kept busy in order to stay alive. One was the cook, one the foreman, one in charge of water. And one miner was the poet. His job, I'd like to imagine, was the most important. I can hear his words vibrate the rock, drill bits turning and turning, incantations boring a hole toward the sky.

Crush

Years ago, on the island of Santorini, I walked the village at sunrise, gazing at vineyards that grow differently there—close to the ground, like mounded beans, rather than the upright regiments I knew in California. In Greece, the grapes sprawl in leisure, indifferent to the future. Or not indifferent, but plump with it, glad to be turned to a greater purpose. I always want to be there, in that village at dawn; I want to be those grapes beholden to the wine, born to a pleasure that comes only after the crush.

How to Get Ready for Bed

Lately your back hurts when you wake, a grabbing pain that locks up your hips and lower back. Your doctor tests your reflexes (it still gives you a little thrill, the way your leg kicks out so spritely on its own), and he says, *It's probably your bed.* Your mattress is only ten years old; you thought a bed was supposed to last longer, this bed you bought when you first moved into that tiny house by the bay: a double not a queen, a bed big enough really only for one. It still looks new enough: no stains, no sags, no tears, but your doc tells you it's the *inside* that matters: things wear out in ways we can't really see.

So you go to the sleep shop in the groovy part of town—locally owned, expensive brands—just to check it out, just to see what the difference could possibly be between a $600 mattress and a $3000 mattress. You lie down on Tempurpedic, Englander, Beauty Rest. You try pillow tops and Eurotops and super plush tops. On some of these mattresses they've placed a clear plastic cube to reveal a cross-section of the interior, to show what remains hidden: the coils and springs, or the layers of various types of foam. You don't really understand what you're looking at, but you nod anyway, test the bed's firmness with the palm of your hand.

You know you're supposed to lie on a prospective bed in your preferred sleep position for at least half an hour, a feat that can be difficult in the showroom, with its fluorescent lights, the plate glass window, and the salesman who keeps hovering. But you try it. You slip off your snow boots and your jacket, realize you forgot to get dressed this morning: you're still wearing the sweatpants you slept in, and the long-sleeved t-shirt without a bra. All the better, you think, to test out this bed.

You crawl onto the Eurotop and turn onto your belly, bring one knee up in your typical half fetal position and close your eyes. But the salesman is there; he even kneels on the bed and jumps a little to show you how steady the mattress will remain even with someone else tossing and turning. He keeps saying that most beds wear out because of the combined weight of sleepers compressing the coils and foam. *But that won't be a problem for you*, he says, eyeing your slim hips, missing the Buddha belly hidden by your fleece.

Don't respond. Try to pretend you're just sleeping, your breath growing deeper, drifting off to sleep the way you normally do; if you were simulating this accurately you would prop yourself up with three pillows and read until the book drops to your chest and your snore startles you awake enough to turn on your side, arrange the full body pillow under your knees.

You imagine a whole store full of bed shoppers arriving in their robes and slippers, husbands and wives side by side with their itty-bitty reading lights; single men in their boxer shorts; children with their stuffed animals; the single women with their night masks, mouth-guards, moisturizing gloves. You imagine the couples reaching a hand to a thigh, a mouth to an ear. Because wouldn't this be the ultimate test of a bed and what it can withstand, something you'd want to know before plunking down a couple thousand bucks? How this bed would feel under the weight of two bodies, not in the prim awkward contortions of sleep, but pressed together, in rhythm—how much resistance would you need, how much support? Do you want memory foam that absorbs everything? A bed that *remembers* you, a curvature that aligns with every knob and bone? Perhaps not. Perhaps memory is exactly the opposite of what you need when making love.

Remember the bed you had years ago, in Montana, in a tiny studio apartment that cost $298 a month? It was a bed-in-a-drawer that pulled out from a sideboard cabinet, with a squeaky mattress that had probably not been changed since 1928. You loved that bed. Well, not the bed itself, but the feeling it gave you of sleeping in a children's story, as if at any moment that bed would roll itself back into the drawer, with you on board, and you'd find yourself in a fantastical land, a whole world that existed behind the lathe and plaster. Your boyfriend lived in an apartment below yours, and often you lay in that bed late at night, listening for his footstep in the hall.

Later, when you lived together in Seattle, this boyfriend built you a bed. He built the frame in one day with wood trucked home from the lumber yard, assembling it in the bedroom, screwing the sanded planks together with a cordless drill. He moved quickly, expertly, the muscles in his forearms tense, sweat filming on the back of his neck. He wore denim cutoffs and a thin white T-shirt, a Hanes Beefy-T; you watched him from the doorway as he measured the raw planks, like Figaro measuring the space of his marriage bed, so intent on his work he remained unaware of your presence—oblivious, as men in labor often are.

You were drawn most to the movement of his wrists. On your first date, you kept your gaze focused on those wrists as he ate his burger, drank his beer; those wrists were tapered and delicate, and you imagined, even then, kissing them, placing your lips softly against his pulse. As you watched him build your bed, it seemed that all the force of this construction hinged there in the wrist—as he picked up the screw gun, held it tightly against the joint, put it down, swiveled on his knees for more nails, more wood, a piece of sandpaper, those quick hard swipes. Dust hung in the air around him, floated out the open window. You remember thinking this meant something: that somehow those hands built not only a bed, but a marriage, a solid place you could dwell in together without a thought.

The bed frame, it turned out, would be too big, too solid, too heavy— impossible to move from that room. Before your boyfriend left, he had to split it in two with his circular saw. You didn't watch. You lay with eyes closed in the hammock outside. But you heard the high whine of the saw as it bit into the frame, smelled the raw pine, pungent and new, as if the wood that had suffered beneath the two of you all those years had never aged, and all along kept some memory of its own beginnings.

∾

The salesman's voice brings you out of your reverie and back into the showroom. He's looming above you, with his white beard, his nervous hands. He needs to make a sale. He asks, a little too loudly, *Do you have a sleep partner?* A sleep partner? You hesitate a moment, have never thought of it this way, a *sleep partner.* You haven't had a sleep partner in many years, have not had to conform your body to the sleep posture of another. It seems an oddly intimate question, in a situation already fraught with false and awkward intimacy. You are bra-less and vulnerable. You haven't washed your hair.

You want to blurt out, *It's none of your business*—though you know he's asking just as a matter of fact, so that he can tell you more about springs and coils and the way a couple's weight can distribute most efficiently over a bed's wide surface. So you murmur, your eyes still closed, *Not at the moment*, implying that you're just *between* sleep partners right now, that any minute now a sleep partner might arrive, easily as a tennis partner in a doubles match, dressed for the sport, racket in hand.

This can include four-legged partners, he adds quickly, seeing his mistake, backtracking, and you smile in your fake sleep, and say, *Well, in that case, there's my dog and my cat*—both of whom don't really share your bed, but allow you to occupy it with them. Your dog is waiting in the car, and you briefly consider going to get her, to lift her onto the bed with you, to simulate exactly this going-to-bed routine. She would snuffle around your head, and then sniff every corner of the mattress before plopping down at your feet, head on her paws, eyes staring at you to gauge what moves you will make now.

Your bed is actually quite crowded and would never hold the three of you *plus* a sleep partner of the two-legged variety. So maybe you will go for it, get the queen-sized mattress which is priced to lure you into thinking it's the better deal, though it will mean so many other new purchases too (as these things always do): new bed frame, new duvet, new linens. The salesman says, *It's been shown that people sleep better in a bigger bed*—but you don't understand how that has been shown and who showed it; you don't understand why that would be the case when, in your bed, you take up such a small sliver of real estate.

And now you sit up on the edge of the bed, look around this store: Sleep Solutions, it's called, as if sleep were a complex mathematical problem to be solved. And it *is* a problem, you realize now: so many equations to balance in order to get a good night's sleep.

Your doctor tells you that you need better "sleep hygiene," an admonition that makes you blush; it puts you right back in the pediatrician's office, the nurse's office, the school auditorium—where the word "hygiene" took on vaguely sordid connotations. "Feminine hygiene products": they passed out samples you hid in your knapsack. *Sleep hygiene* makes you want to sniff your underarms, but the good doctor is merely talking about all those positive things one is supposed to do as you get ready for bed: a cup of soothing tea, a good book, no email, no TV, no Internet. You have to really *get ready* for bed, as if it were an event; you have to signal that you're moving from one mode of being to another. You have to treat yourself like a toddler who needs the discipline of routine.

Your sleep hygiene is horrendous: you'll surf the net for hours until you can't even keep your eyes open. You'll keep eating cereal. You'll get so tired you can barely brush your teeth, much less wash your face, apply the many moisturizers a woman your age has lined up in the bathroom cabinet. You don't even put on pajamas; you wriggle out of your bra and fall into bed in whatever you were wearing. The dog's been there before you, hours before you, and she looks at you balefully as you shove her off your pillow. You've done this every night for years, and still she acts as if your late arrival comes as a surprise. She harrumphs and rolls on her side, her back a curve of reproach.

Once you're under the covers, you close your eyes. You hear the dog snore. The cat appears and asks for her five daily minutes of petting. You comply and then she, too, leaves you to your sliver of bed. You drift off, but then at 3 a.m. you're wide awake. You drift off, you're awake, and this pattern continues until 6 a.m., when the dog and the cat are ready to get up—*they* have had an excellent night's sleep, thank you very much. You go through the rest of the day exhausted, but still find yourself at your desk at midnight, surfing the Internet for a new pair of shoes. It's as if you're afraid of something, but you don't know what. Maybe you're afraid of that moment you slip from knowing to unknowing—the moment you're with your unpartnered self alone.

You promised the doctor you'd do better from now on; you have to solve this sleep problem; you have to pay attention to the literal pain in your ass that grabs you when waking. Shopping for this new mattress is the first step, but there are too many choices here, too many facts, too many dollar signs. The salesman stands by the window wringing his hands. It snowed last night, and the sidewalks are covered in ice, so he won't have many customers today.

The salesman had high hopes for you; you kept patting the mattresses, saying, *This one feels great.* You don't want to disappoint him, but now you feel worn through every layer; a cross section of your insides would show battered coils and springs.

So don't buy anything yet. And as you step carefully back to your car—to the waiting dog and her hopeful eyes—you think about your bedroom as a child: how sanctified it was, how you shut the door and felt the room come toward you, friendly, saying: *here you are, here you are, here you are.* Even now you remember every inch of that room—with its nubby white bedspread and stiff sheets, the headboard with sliding doors that could hide whatever you wanted to hide. You heard the rest of the house going about its life without you, except when you turned the record player up loud: Simon and Garfunkel's "Bridge Over Troubled Water," or James Taylor's "You've Got a Friend," or Carole King's "I Feel the Earth Move"—and now you wonder what those songs sounded like from outside the door, the faint warbling of a scratched record.

You know your mother must have listened. Your mother must have stood with an ear tilted toward your room, trying to get some sense of what her mute daughter thought—what she *felt*—during all those solitary hours she shut herself in alone, humming along, eyes closed, to songs that begged for friendship, for connection.

Or you think even further back, getting ready for bed as a child: you always knew just what to do and when to do it—brush your teeth, put on your pajamas—and then always a story, always your mother's body close to yours, tucked in, in the twin bed: not going anywhere, nowhere to go but to sleep.

❧

Now, forty-odd years later, you imagine the bedroom you'll eventually create: a mattress that loves your body, cradled in a *real* bed frame, something modern but a little old-fashioned: maybe a sleigh of polished cherry that holds you through the night. Perhaps you'll even spring for that wildly expensive duvet cover you've been coveting at the home décor place downtown—lush white cotton embellished with gray branches and tawny finches. *Chinoiserie*, they call it: the flora and fauna inked on with a calligrapher's touch.

This comforter would truly be a comfort. This bed will tell you *it's okay*, no matter how you've passed the night, no matter how scared or sweaty or bruised. Your bed will confirm: *you've chosen well*. It will assuage: *your life is not cold*. It will urge: *listen to these birds as they wake*—birds who call and call, always sure that some other bird will answer.

Be More

I'm sorry I gave it away, that nightstand you made for me so many years ago. Well you didn't really make it; you revised it. You found the battered table at a garage sale, saw the potential (its "good bones," as you often said of imperfect things), and somehow—in secret, in the basement—sanded the wood down, puttied every hole, fixed the drawer, and added a shim to make it level. You shellacked it all a deep black, then attached an unusual drawer pull: a wooden goddess—a Thai flying angel.

In those days, over twenty years ago, such ornaments swarmed the import stores in Seattle: multi-colored women with finely cut wings, their chests bowed up, like figureheads on a ship. Their faces were tiny and exquisite, chins cleft like espresso beans. Some steady hand had painted them, drawing lines of vermillion, emerald, and gold flake across those stiff and supple bodies. Their eyes always fluttered closed, their full lips fell slightly apart: an expression that could be taken as either saintly or hinting at sin.

You must have gone into that store we liked in Wallingford, the one that smelled of rosewood and jasmine, stuffed full of wool serapes, tie-dyed scarves, dolls of coconut shell. The goddesses must have flocked above you, each one bobbing on a string, slowly turning. I imagine you stood for several moments in their sway, surrounded by this horde of outlandish women. How could you pick just one?

This angel drew your eye: a woman who seemed to arc up from the sea, her back morphing to a mermaid's tail. A woman half-wild, a woman so different from me. Me, in my turtleneck shirts, my rumpled khakis that never fit quite right. Me, who blushed whenever you studied me in that appraising way.

You took the chosen one home, performed your secret work, then wrapped the finished nightstand in Christmas paper, presented it with the glee one takes in the perfect gift: your eyes eagerly on mine to see them alight when I discovered the hidden woman inside. But I must have disappointed you: my eyes flickering in doubt before putting on the expected delight. The nightstand *was* beautiful, amazing even, and I exclaimed at how and when you'd created such a thing without my knowing it.

But that woman. There was something about her that seemed a reproach rather than a blessing. Her turquoise breasts so perfect, so proud, the body curved like an offering, the way that every time I opened the drawer I would need to encircle her tiny waist with my index finger. Something in her pose seemed to be your proxy, saying to me yet again: *Be more.* Be more sexy, more beautiful, more wild. Bare your breasts. Wisecrack at the moon. And now this woman would hover like a hummingbird next to our bed every night, her breasts catching your eye as you spooned against the same old me.

It wasn't long before we sat on that bed, a foot apart, the angel a silent witness while we spoke a sad truth that had finally grown immutable. I turned toward the angel, covered my eyes with one hand. I wished I were someone else then, someone who could remain solid, moving through the world with my heart splendidly forward.

For years after we split up, I kept that nightstand by my bed. You'd made it well: the paint stayed smooth and the goddess never loosened her grip. It moved from house to house, state to state; I wrapped the goddess carefully in bubble wrap, and she took up her post next to me in my sleep. Once, her nose got chipped, making her a little less lovely, awkward and out of joint, but still she kept that smug, sexy look on her face. She never had a backache. She never got headaches. She just kept bending upward. And those breasts—god, those breasts! They just never quit. I passed those breasts every night on my way to sleep, saw them when I closed my eyes, and always I got a flash of you: that face etched with tender disappointment and love.

Until, one day, I stroked the angel's tiny head, tapped an index finger to her full lips, and said, *Be quiet.* I transplanted her upstairs, in a corner out of sight, where I glimpsed her less frequently. She became a spare nightstand for overnight guests, who always exclaimed over her beauty, her cleverness. Sometimes I told them the story and sometimes I didn't. Sometimes I let her speak for herself.

And then, after a while, it became clear to me she needed to go. Maybe it was a book I read about feng shui, the experts telling me that one should never hold onto relics that remind us of a flawed past. We must clear out, they say, de-clutter, make way for whatever will come to us next. And I knew that, even when out of sight, this woman's reproach pulsed through the house. I stood at the foot of the stairs and imagined my life without her.

I couldn't bear to sell her, so one morning I put her out on the curb with a "Free" sign taped on top. I watched from my front window, and in the light from the street I could see her colors had faded. Scratches dulled the surface of the black varnish, and one leg had been damaged, bare wood splintering at the base. I turned away for just a moment, and when I turned back, she was vanishing, wrestled into the back seat of a stranger's car.

I'd known she wouldn't last long out there—such a find, such a treasure—but still it made me gasp, the speed of it, as if I'd just witnessed an abduction.

I turned back to my house. I didn't really feel much different; there were, after all, so many other reminders if I looked for them: a hand-embroidered rug from Turkey we had bought together— after a dozen tiny glasses of tea—from that slick rug merchant in Istanbul; the mirror you'd made for me framed in varnished oak. Even making coffee in the morning, with that little sprinkle of cinnamon on top, became a gesture you'd left behind.

Years passed, as they do, and I really didn't think about the Thai goddess too much. I bought a new bed, and twin nightstands from an online import store. These tables are simple and lovely in their own way: blond teak, with drawers that slide smoothly on their runners. They hold no history. All this furniture is blank-faced, innocent; all of it matches too well.

What I now know—and what I wished I'd known then—is that we really can't toss away this evidence of our past; it's like putting yourself out on the curb and taping a free sign to your chest. And we are not rubbish, not one part of us. I'd been the one wagging my *own* finger in reproach; the goddess—she'd meant no harm.

If I had her back to keep me company, I might be able to turn on my side and gaze at that injured woman, reach out a finger to stroke her aging body. If I could reclaim her, I'd touch this woman's closed eyes, her chapped lips, her craggy wings. I'd feel every indentation, the ridges of her against my fingerprints. I'd be able to say, and mean it, *You're beautiful.* I'd murmur, *Thank you for the gift* as I drifted off to sleep.

The Single Girl's Guide
to Remodeling

I

For five years, be perfectly content with the small breakfast nook off the kitchen, the rickety back porch, the galley kitchen with its ancient linoleum. Remain enamored of your 1920s bungalow, with a huge backyard, a cherry tree in that yard, window boxes full of pansies that seem to last even through the snow. Train yourself to ignore the house's flaws; after a brief spate of home improvement—a new circuit box, a new water heater, Berber carpet in the bedroom—relegate to a back room the inspection report with all its "major concerns" and "safety issues" bristling in red ink.

When you have dinner parties, it will be perfectly reasonable to squat around the coffee table in the living room, carefully cutting slices of brisket or forking up roast chicken. Ignore your friends' children spilling grape juice or grinding crumbs into the sofa cushions. Ignore the recycling bin in the corner of the breakfast nook, the accumulation of bags and other persistent litter between the stove and refrigerator. You clean up the best you can, but at some point, the house resists cleaning.

Accept this. You know that when people enter your house, they do not notice the lopsided doorway or the cracked windowpane in the kitchen door or the wobble of the kitchen chairs. They do not see the shredded legs of your couch, the impossible mess that has accumulated in the linen closet.

Your guests seem to notice only the gold mosaic of a Buddha head on your living-room wall. They notice the healthy houseplants, the cherry tree (when it's in bloom). They often comment on how "serene" the house feels to them, how relaxing, a comment that both pleases and surprises you, since serenity is, after all, your decorating scheme, with all your Zen accents, the calligraphy by Thich Nhat Hanh in the hallway—"I have arrived, I am home"—the bamboo in the corner to hide the television cables and cords.

But at the same time you know you've constructed a detailed façade, a false front, like the ones you saw on the Wild West sets as a kid when you and your family toured Universal Studios: saloon doors, the wide window of a dry-goods store, log walls, all hiding a suite of ordinary buildings. When you turned the corner, you could see how flat it all really was, how insubstantial. Your guests don't know to look in the crowded drawers, the cluttered cupboards, the back room you've come to call "the room of shame."

II

At about the five-year mark, the honeymoon will be over. Your gas furnace will quit at the same time as your washing machine. Things will begin to expire, as if in agreement with one another. The chimney of the nonworking fireplace loses its stucco, and the bricks appear to be skewed, ready to fall on an unsuspecting pedestrian. You need more insulation in the attic, you admit, lying in bed, your teeth chattering. During a particularly aggressive rainstorm, the basement floods, and the sump pump decides not to work; old cartons float by, then a flowerpot with a dried-up dahlia.

You dig out that inspection report, stare at it, make half-hearted notes in the margin: an asterisk here, an exclamation point there. There's the question of the foundation, some old insect damage at the front of the house, a "major concern." There's the missing railing on the basement steps, a "safety issue." The pipes will freeze on your washing machine overnight, then burst in the morning, a flood on the back porch.

Luckily you have a neighbor, a single woman like you, who can lend an ear in commiseration. You call her in a panic when the pipes break, and she keeps watch while you try to find the water shut-off valve in the basement, in a crawl space sticky with cobwebs.

You like your neighbor and she likes you. You go over to one another's houses to assess a new rug, a wall color, yet another pair of boots. You feed one another's cats; you call one another for boyfriend interventions. You bring her soup; she brings you canned salmon. You raid each other's Netflix stashes. She likes to call out, *Howdy neighbor!* when she sees you come out your back door. You've named your duo "The Single Woman's Housing Co-op," with your communal wheelbarrow, ladder, snow shovel, raised garden bed. There are no fences between you.

When her cat is dying, she'll come to your door, her face twisted, saying, *Cooper's sick, something's wrong.* You will go quickly to her house, where her big, friendly cat, Cooper, lies on her back porch, sitting in his own feces, mewling a sick cry that makes you wince. Without a moment's hesitation, you drive them to the animal hospital, where you put your arm around your friend as the vet takes x-rays. *It looks like poison*, he says. You drive your neighbor home with the soiled towel in her lap. When you call her in the morning, she tells you Cooper died in the night. You tell her how much you loved Cooper, how you would often find him on your porch, or in your car, ready to have a chat. She buries him in the backyard, and you watch her put a small statue of a cat where Cooper rests in peace.

When you have what you will come to call your "heart episode," your neighbor sits with you for hours in the trauma room at the hospital, making jokes about the cute medics, helping you interpret the doctors' brusque comments. When they say you have to spend the night, she will hold your hand when you cry, those big silent tears rolling down your cheeks. *Don't worry*, she says. *I'll take care of everything.*

III

Once you decide you need to make some changes, it's difficult to know where to begin. It's almost a full-time job maintaining a house by yourself, and you already have a full-time job. You get out the Yellow Pages. You make some calls. You have men coming to your house putting on little booties over their dirty work shoes. You're nodding your head at whatever they say. They ask if you have any questions, and you don't even know what questions to ask. You go online, join chat forums, try to educate yourself, but all this knowledge seems to dissolve the minute you're confronted with a man wearing a low-slung tool belt.

Be prepared to find out that, no matter what you plan to do with the house, it always costs $1,500. New furnace? $1,500. New back steps? $1,500. New skylight in the attic? $1,500. New brick chimney built up from the eaves? Hmmm, let's see: $1,500. It's one of the first mysteries you encounter as a homeowner: how so many wildly different procedures can cost exactly the same amount of money. Plus tax.

Be prepared for the fact that money will take on a different dimension. Money no longer seems yours to have and to hold, but more like a child on a roller coaster—up and down, up again, and then the giddy, scream-inducing descent. It won't stay put. It always wants to go for another ride.

IV

One autumn you need to have the cherry tree cut down; it's too sickly, too at risk for falling. But you'll cringe every time you drive into the carport and see the freshly cut stump. You'll walk to the edge of your backyard, then look at the house, notice all the peeling paint and broken siding the tree's shadow had hidden.

It's time for a change. You need something different in your life. A new relationship, even if it's just with your house.

But what kind of change? The foundation work that always lurks in your conscience? Or new plumbing that you know must be necessary in this old house, with its temperamental drains? But those things are so invisible, so *dowdy*. What you really want is the dining room that's been taking shape in your mind, you realize now, ever since you stepped foot in this house.

A real dining room. Big enough to seat ten. With a pantry that will hide the recycling, the brooms, all the pet food and supplies. A dining room open to the kitchen, where your friends will gather. They will chat with you while you cook. You eye the back wall with its picture window, a wall that now seems simple to demolish.

You consult with the dog, who looks up at you from her bed, head cocked to the side. She seems to say, *Whatever you want, Boss.* You consult the tarot cards, the *I-Ching*, your horoscope. If you had a Magic 8 Ball you would shake it and know this message would appear: "All Signs Point to Yes."

V

Hire your contractor based on just one recommendation from Angie's List. Angie's List was made, it seems, for people just like you: Single women who are looking for the right men. A different kind of Match.com.

You read about your contractor—a team of two brothers—the rave review about how nice they are, how thorough, how efficient. You look them up, and like their website. You like the way they pose with their families, all of them good-looking and happy.

Dave has a nice voice on the phone. He sounds like someone you can talk to. He seems like he wouldn't rip off a single woman, something that you know would be so easy to do, given your apparent cluelessness about the simplest things. Dave comes over and promises he can do the job to fit your budget, and it will take about a month. *Deal*, you say, and so you begin telling people you're going to do it, finally, the remodeling that's been in your mind all this time.

Everyone warns you that any big job takes twice as long, and will cost at least thirty percent more than you're quoted. Don't listen to them. Dave was so nice. And so tall. That won't happen to you. So you sign the refinance papers, take out your cash—$25,000 (*smart*, you think, *a little buffer*)—and sign the multi-page contracts.

VI

You've had enough experience with painting to understand that you really don't know how to pick the right colors by looking at a paint chip, have never had the patience to sample colors on a wall before buying gallons of the wrong paint. Seek out Ruthie V., an artist. When she arrives at your door, she looks avid for the task ahead. Her eyes are wide and take in everything. She wears quirky glasses you covet. As you tour the existing rooms in the house, she asks which colors you like and why. Say something unexpected: *I chose this color because it's unassuming but bright.*

Like you, she says, smiling.

When you enter the construction zone, Ruthie's gaze travels across the wide expanse of lawn, rests on your elderly neighbor's plum tree by the back fence. The tree's branches, barren of fruit, still radiate a dark, reddish purple through the leaves. *That's it*, she will say, *that's the color we need to bring into this room.*

Really? you will say. *But I don't want pink.*

Don't worry, it won't come out pink, she says. Then she points to your shirt, your living-room rug, the throw pillow on the couch. All of them beating out *plum, plum, plum.*

VII

I know a guy, you tell the brothers. You can see they don't like this phrase, have heard it before, and would prefer to work with their own people. *But really . . . you'll like him, and he knows my house.* This seems important to you, to have someone on this team who already knows your house intimately, who won't be surprised by its flaws. He was the one to rewire the entire attic when you put insulation in last winter. He was the one who carried out truckloads of junk from the crawl space under the eaves before he could begin the rewiring, junk dating back from the twenties, stuff you had no idea was lurking there: an old radio, boxes and boxes of hand-lettered receipts, a fortune-telling paper doll.

He lives right up the street. He's a neighbor. And besides, he's single, he reads Buddhist texts, and he's fun to have around.

The brothers relent. You call up the electrician, and he's happy for the work. It turns out all these men will get along famously; they'll talk and talk while working together, long conversations about politics, movies, and, most surprisingly, relationships. They'll go out for beer after work, to talk about what it's like to be men—married or single, together or alone. You didn't know men could talk this way. You'll feel a little left out of the party, but you won't sulk. You'll keep smiling gamely as they work on remodeling your life.

VIII

Be prepared to make a *lot* of decisions, even after the main choice has been made. You thought you could relax, but there will be a hundred things to decide before the job is done. Making decisions involves so many complex neurological tasks—it's called a "decision tree": a hundred tiny twigs quivering, synapses firing with every turn that a real decision requires. Ever since you learned about the decision tree, you can't help imagining it as a huge, towering maple, like the one in front of your yoga teacher's house, more than a hundred years old and still growing. When you do tree pose at this house, you turn yourself to face this maple, to feel its ancient roots tenaciously holding ground.

But when it comes to making decisions, you feel all the branches quivering when you look at the plans, two-dimensional drawings that are supposed to tell you everything you need to know—square footage, trusses, pitch of the roof, where the doorways will go, windows, depth of foundation, and all those etceteras—but in actuality do not tell you all the things you *really* want to know, such as how the light will fall at 7 p.m. as you finish your dinner and linger a few moments at the table; or the light at 7 a.m. as you stand on the deck with your coffee, watching the full moon set behind a bank of quickly breaking clouds.

IX

Despite all the planning—the well-worn blueprints, the murmured readjustments—when the building starts, you'll be surprised to see where the walls are going up—one of them right in front of your office window—and how small the dining room looks, and the deck, is it really going to be only a few feet wide? The laundry-room door seems too narrow, and, *Tell me again about the pantry—how that will work?* You feel that little tremble in your lip, as if you're about to start crying, but you don't want to start crying—it would embarrass all of you.

Luckily you have nice contractors. Contractors who are cute and tall and listen to NPR while they work, not heavy metal or rock and roll. They smile and gesture and never raise their voices as they answer your questions and wait for you to tell them what to do. They often say things such as, *Well, we're trying to stay within your budget*, but not unkindly, just as a matter of fact. In the end, you say, again, *Whatever you think is best*, because the more you research and monitor online forums about remodeling and look at magazines and ask your friends, the more confused you become. In this case, knowledge is not power. It is barely even knowledge.

They go back to work, tell you a funny story, seem to hardly notice the decision tree dropping its dead leaves. The decision tree has taken the place of the Rainier cherry, though its shade is not so delicate and its fruit—so far—not as sweet.

X

They've demolished the back porch, dug and poured the foundation, demolished the back wall, built up new walls, laid sheetrock and layers of mud. They've done all this behind a translucent sheet stretched across your kitchen, which silhouettes their figures and makes them ghostly as you make your coffee and eat your cereal in the living room each morning. You listen to your NPR station while they listen to theirs. You hear them talking about their children, their wives, the activities they did over the weekend; they talk in those smooth rhythms of family, and for a while there, in the mornings, you will kind of feel like part of their family—not a daughter exactly, or a wife, but a cousin, a cousin who has come to visit, a cousin who doesn't want to leave.

Throughout your remodeling, post pictures of the process on Facebook. People who normally don't talk to you at all—your colleagues at work, in particular—suddenly begin stopping you in the hallways to ask about paint colors, foundations, and countertops. This puzzles you for a minute, until you realize they've been watching you from their computers. This fact will both please and distress you, so you keep posting the pictures and hover near the computer to see who will "like" them. Look for approval wherever it might be found.

XI

One day, Dave will bring you an invoice for the work done so far. The minute he parts the translucent veil to get to you, you see he's wearing his sheepish look, and you brace yourself. Dave hates to disappoint, and you hate to be disappointed. *Well*, he says, *we're coming in a little high*, and he shows you the bill, with figures on it that seem impossibly large. He promises to cut labor costs in half to at least come back into the ballpark of the original estimate, but that ballpark, you think, must be bigger than Yankee Stadium.

It's time, anyway, to link together the kitchen and dining room, so the veil comes down; the paintbrushes come out. *I can help*, you say, hoping to keep the costs at a minimum, and so for the next several weeks you will become the brothers' slave. You will do whatever they ask: spend hours painting the teal cabinets white, strain your eyes to touch up the yellow in the corners, prowl the dining room with a thin brush to perfect that plum. You paint doors, you paint trim, you attach door pulls and knobs. You surprise yourself with all you can do.

You work side by side, mostly with Dave, and you fall into that easy rhythm of murmured conversation. You hear a song on the radio, and you both say, *That's a blast from the past*, or, *That's an interesting version of the song*, the way a couple might talk at the breakfast table, saying things to one another that are not really endearments, but which have that endearing quality to them. Then you hear, in the background, David Byrne singing, *How did I get here?* and, *This is not my beautiful wife, this is not my beautiful house*, and you both start humming it, and Dave might start telling you about his many incarnations—as a helicopter pilot, a fisherman, an engineer—and then you just stop talking, the way couples do, both of you engrossed in the painting, while outside, his brother works the circular saw.

XII

As the brothers near completion, you begin to feel a little nervous. You've grown accustomed to their faces, as the old song says, *Grown accustomed to the trace of something in the air.*

You know that you'll miss these men in your house, tall men who know how to use hammers and saws, who can envision a room where none exists, who can build from the ground up, make sturdy foundations and walls and ceilings. You'll miss the big trucks in your driveway—one white and one green—the male energy in the house, all these men working so hard to please you, to make you happy.

Prepare yourself now for the emptiness that will come when they're gone. You'll miss these men in their smelly work clothes, calling out good morning, cranking up NPR, chatting, mulling over the plans, peering intently at your walls, pouring attention onto your house and so, by extension, onto you. Admit that you found yourself falling in love with them a little bit—if love means that warm companionship you feel as you're painting a cabinet cloud-white while he fixes the hinges.

You're driving home one day and realize you're behind Dave's truck. You see the back of his head, his hand tapping the steering wheel. You understand that he's going to your house, too, and you feel unreasonably giddy.

One day, Dave will peek his head in the door and say, *Well, that's it, we're done*, and you'll say, *Okay, see you tomorrow*, until you realize he means done *for good.*

XIII

When people come over to see the new parts of your house, they often utter the phrase, *You've done such a good job!* You protest: *But I didn't do any of it. It was all the men!* Slowly you come to realize that you *did* do a good job, that you are a part of these details. You envisioned it, you made all those decisions, you hired the right people.

You'll wake with your familiar aches and pains, hold one hand to the small of your back as you make your coffee, the dog already at the back door waiting to be let out. She skitters on the damp planks that still smell like cedar. You step out with her in your worn slippers to look across the expanse of green that now seems so much more . . . how do you put it? So much more *yours*.

XIV

Fall arrives, and you invite your best friends to celebrate Suzanne's birthday. You'll make foods you've never made before: *mulligatawny*, zucchini meatballs, sweet-and-sour tamarind sauce. You extend one end of the table, set it with flowers and candles, soup bowls and plates. Your friends will arrive with their dog, and your dog, Abbe, will perk up in a way you haven't seen her do for months. The two dogs will circle all the people in the living room, then settle under the table, like a scene from a painting called *Dinner Party with Dogs*.

The new dining room somehow makes the kitchen bigger, the whole house bigger, big enough to hold all your friends and then some. They mill around the homemade *papadam* Lee brought, dipping it in the tamarind sauce that tastes so complex you can't help but keep sampling it again and again, trying to discern all the flavors. *Raisins*, you finally tell them, *it's made with raisins*. And ginger, and cinnamon, and tamarind, so many flavors marrying together without even being cooked.

You serve the *mulligatawny* from the stove, but all the other dishes are arrayed on the table, because now there is plenty of room. People can pass platters along, heap servings onto plates, and all the while they are talking, talking, talking, and laughing. At some point you'll let the dogs out in the backyard, and because your yard is still not fenced, you stay out there on the deck to watch them until they're ready to come back inside. Night has fallen—an early autumn night, with its cool touch to the air, the light farther south than it's been all summer, still a thin blue line on the horizon.

While you wait, you turn back to the house and see, through that enormous glass door, your dinner party going on without you, lit by the unobtrusive recessed lights, the candles in their Pier One metal boat. You watch your friends laughing, eating, bent over their plates and scooping up kale with mango, *roti* with raita, the platters continually passed. Someone's wine glass is always in the air, mid-drink. Ed leans back in his chair, and his hands are waving; you know he is telling a funny story, and you wait for it, wait for it . . . and there it is—the perfectly timed burst of laughter from all of them, a hand slapped on the table, as someone else wipes away tears.

Their children are not here this evening: Sofie already a young woman, working her weekend job at the pizzeria; Jin a new teenager, thirteen years old, who would rather now be with his friends on a Saturday night. They've been here for many Hanukkahs, many birthdays, sitting on the floor in the living room with their plates, playing their Gameboys together, swapping game cards and strategies. But now they seem to be going on without you, and the parents take this in stride most of the time, understand the children won't be with them forever. You watch your friends without their children, talking and talking. Your house is filled with their voices. You're outside looking in, your friends making a backlit tableau, a picture of family that replaces the one you once thought mandatory.

You turn back to check on the dogs, who are walking circles in the middle of the lawn, noses deep into the weeds. And now Abbe stops, looks at you though you haven't said a word. Meeko comes running first, and Abbe follows, the two of them galumphing up the steps and making a beeline toward their people.

XV

Your house, now that you've changed it, seems capable of even more change. You move through the house, away from the perfect dining room, and you start eyeing the lopsided doorway in the living room, the small bathroom with its ugly texture on the upper walls.

You begin to surreptitiously cruise the Internet for new bathroom sinks and fancy faucets. You understand now the adrenaline rush of change, and you eye the kitchen counters, think, *Maybe granite.* It would be nice to see the brothers again; there must be some job you can rustle up to lure them back, some way to squirrel away the money. You feel like a junkie, and you pull away from that edge, give yourself a bone: just that new sink in the bathroom, that's all, just one couldn't hurt. And maybe a counter that wraps across the top of the toilet. And maybe shelves, but *that's it!* Still you know there's really no end to it, no end to what can be changed.

All this time, you know what you *really* want is to feel that kind of renovation going on in yourself—a complete gut job from the inside out—but such a project involves unforeseen obstacles, and dust, lots of dust, living with a mess for a while as you demolish and start all over again. You'll have to call in some experts, be patient as they look you over, survey your old wiring, the hazardous foundation. They'll say, *This is what we can do,* and provide estimates that you know will be wholly inaccurate.

You think about all this as you cruise Overstock.com for your new sink. You think about this as you're holding up yet more paint chips against the ugly bathroom wall, and maybe you'll ask Dave if that texture can be changed, *while we're at it,* a phrase that you know is dangerous, that leads you into all kinds of trouble.

So you turn off the computer, and get out your yoga mat. You close your eyes and bend into child's pose, breathing deeply. You feel the house go quiet around you—the fridge humming in its new corner, the dining room blushing with pleasure. You try to remember what it's like to be content with what is, to not have to change a thing.

Full Service

M y father pulls the station wagon into the Shell station off Devonshire, rolling the car over the thin cords—*ding ding!* A sound I love, a sound that says: *We're here.* A lanky boy comes out with a rag in hand, leans his head toward my father's window, and my father says, *Fill it up with premium and check the oil please.* Full service: even the sound of the phrase is tinged with pleasure. Full. Service.

I watch from the passenger side of the upholstered bench seat, the car smelling musty of old cigarette smoke. I watch the boy in his grimy blue coveralls, the patch on the right shoulder that spells out "Bill" or "Toby" in white cursive. He clunks the pump into place, then pops the hood with expert fingers. *Oil's good*, he says, and even comes over to show my father the dipstick, cradling it with the rag before wiping it clean. He cleans the windows, too, with a few squeaking swipes of the squeegee, rubbing at errant drops with a paper towel until the windshield is spotless, while my father rummages in his wallet for the Shell credit card.

His wallet is full of credit cards for every conceivable thing—three gas stations, Sears, The Broadway, American Express, MasterCard—and always cash he keeps track of in a little book. There's another little book in the glove box, and he leans over me to get it, writes down the mileage and the number of gallons we'll take this time, the car chugging them down while the boy stands now with one hand on the pump, the other on top of the car, foot resting on the curb; he smells of oil, gasoline, and licorice, and I love him.

I close my eyes, waiting for the click that will tell us we're done, the clunk of the pump withdrawn and muscled back into place, the squeak of the gas cap as he squinches it closed. He comes back with my father's credit card on a little clipboard, and my father signs the slip with a scrawl. I'm only a witness to this transaction between men: the older man so practiced, so sure, in control of this car and its cargo; the younger man confident of his tasks and how to do them well. He wipes his hands on his pants, then glances quickly at me and grins. I turn my face away, suddenly hot, until he walks back inside, going wherever boys go when you're not looking at them.

In a few years' time, when I start driving, the Shell credit card will be the first bit of plastic in my wallet, handed to me by my father as a kind of talisman: a passport to being an adult, to being safe in a world that hides so many obstacles; I'll pull it out as a boy fills up my Pinto, with regular, not premium, and I'll have everything I could ever need. But for now I'm still a passenger, with my face turned toward the window as my father shifts the car into drive. I mouth a goodbye to the boy and his coveralls as we roll slowly out of the gas station, signaling for a left turn onto Devonshire to get wherever we need to go: the hardware store, perhaps. I'm just along for the ride.

Or maybe I'm along for the hot dogs they sell outside the store, from a little cart out front: Kosher dogs roasted on a turning, multi-pronged spit, and the guy hands them to us snuggled in their soft buns. I watch my father squeeze on ketchup and ladle on the relish, onions, and sauerkraut; I eat mine just like his, minus the onions. We sit on a wood-slatted bench in the shade and munch them while the condiments drip into the red-checked paper boat.

We're not in a hurry, my father and I. When we go into the store we're sated on hot dogs and the root beer we shared; this is kind of a secret, because, as my mother would say, we've *ruined our appetites* for dinner. But appetites, I think, are boundless and wholly un-ruinable, and the hardware store confirms this, with aisles and aisles of things one can buy: useful things, necessary things, and things that might come in handy one day. And there are people to help you: grizzled men in vests with names like "Harry" or "Dick" stitched along a patch, men who know the difference between the hundreds of bolts and screws and drill bits that lie about in plastic drawers. I run my hands through a bin of penny-inch nails just to feel their dusty, metallic surfaces.

We check out with the older woman at the cash register—"Sally" or "Gladys"—and get back in the station wagon, hot now from sitting outside so long on the asphalt, and begin the journey home: our bellies full, our car oiled and gassed up, little paper bags filled with useful implements rattling on the seat beside me.

Years later, I'll watch from the passenger seat as my father groans his way out of the car to fill it up himself, because no one helps you anymore—it's all self-serve. You're expected to do everything yourself, your only interaction with a dim screen that's hard to read in the sunlight. He shades his eyes to see *Slide Your Card Here*, flashing on and off, and when he's done, a *Thank You, Please Visit Again* spelled out in bit-mapped letters. My father slips the receipt in his wallet, takes out the little book to mark the mileage and the gallons we've taken, to do the math and see how it all adds up. Before lowering himself back in the car he turns to me—one hand on the windowsill, leaning heavily to keep his balance—and asks if I can drive.

Greyhound

I once got left behind by a Greyhound bus because I'd been
smoking pot in the bathroom. An old man missed the bus, too,
because he'd been swigging Boone's Farm in the men's room—the
two of us now outcast. The bus pulled away from the rest stop,
ignoring us running and waving our arms (the driver had seen
us, I know it, but he kept his jaw in profile, just kept steering that
big bus out of the parking lot), and we stood alone together in the
middle of nowhere.

The two of us walked up onto the freeway ramp toward San
Francisco, stood there and stuck out our thumbs, at the mercy
of traffic flowing south. A woman in a white VW pulled over, a
beautiful woman a little older than me, with long hair and flawless
skin, smelling of jasmine; she leaned over the passenger seat, asked,
Are you with him? She jerked her thumb toward the smelly guy, and
I said, *No*, and then, sheepishly, *Sort of.* I knew the truth: that I was
inexorably linked to this man, he was a part of me now—a deep
down dirty part of me—but I told the woman only about the bus
pulling away, carrying my stuff into the city. The woman said, *Get
in*, and she told the guy to get into the back and *Be quiet*, and we
all drove south for miles.

At first the driver admonished me about the dangers of hitch-
hiking alone, or with characters like *him*, her beautiful brow
furrowed, a frown on her lips, but then she grew gentle, spoke

of her friends in the city, the music they'd play together later that night, the food they would eat. Her voice was like a lullaby, so I could almost imagine, for a moment, that I had a life like this woman's—that I was beautiful and confident, with my own reliable sedan and hair that gathered itself easily into a ponytail, friends waiting for me in a city teeming with strangers.

I could imagine I always knew the right thing to do, like picking up a skinny girl on the highway, a girl so lost she doesn't even know how much danger she's in. I would whip that car to the side of the road, tell her to get in and leave that man behind. *That was close*, I might say, laughing. *A narrow escape.*

We crossed the Golden Gate Bridge—the water alive below us, Alcatraz a gray lump in the haze. We entered that beautiful city, the driver navigating easily through the crowded streets, shifting expertly on the hills. At a corner near the bus station she stopped, turned to the man in the backseat, said, *This is it for you.* He crawled reluctantly out of the car and then turned back to say something, his hand outstretched. I rolled up the window and locked the door.

At that click, he startled, and something changed in his face—a sobering, perhaps, a working of his mouth, his teeth chewing at the inside of his cheek. We locked eyes; I'd never seen anyone so sad, so resigned—on the verge of anger, but an anger directed only at himself. He looked like a car that'd been totaled: damaged just enough so it was no longer worth the trouble and expense to fix.

It was only a moment. I looked away, and he became an anonymous bum again. He shrugged and put his hands deep in his pockets, swaggered down the street. The driver and I looked at each other a long time. She said, *You gonna be all right?* I nodded, then stared out the window silently as she pulled away from the curb.

The Rest of the Story

In the rearview mirror I can see half my mother's face—one lens of her glasses, her right cheek, her right eye as it flicks up toward the mirror to see what's coming up behind. Or to check on me, her only daughter, fifteen years old, sitting quietly—too quietly. My mother's driving is slow, halting; she's a New York girl, subway savvy, navigating this cumbersome station wagon down Californian suburban streets. These streets go in circles and often dead end. Eucalyptus trees, just like ours, grow in so many different yards: always a little tattered, shedding their bark.

When I'm not studying my mother's half face in the rear view, I'm staring cross-eyed at my long hair. Split ends. I unzip them one by one as we bob along, the strands doubling themselves into a fine, wayward frizz until my mother's eye in the mirror catches me and tells me to stop: stop fidgeting, stop scratching, stop splitting, just *stop*. At a red light the car rocks forward and back, the engine idles with its low growl, and my mother lights a cigarette with the electric lighter, pushing in the big knob and then releasing it, carrying that red-hot glowing coal to her mouth.

No seatbelts. No air conditioning. I bend my head to the window, where I can watch the view reflected in the side mirror. I can see the long stretch of Devonshire recede: the shopping mall, the IHOP, the dentist's office—all of them sliding into view in reverse. It's like reversing time, and I wonder if my mother ever wishes for such a thing: a do-over. To start again, marrying someone else, having different children: Am I the daughter she wanted to bear?

I don't know why I think this. My mother seems happy enough, and we like each other, especially at times like this, alone in the car, the car like a miniature house, filled with all the things we might ever need: Kleenex, chewing gum, stuffed animals, food, water, coffee, books, crayons, paper, and the radio tuned to the AM station with Paul Harvey telling us *The Rest of the Story.*

Perhaps it's because my parents have recently taken me to a family therapist, the kind who believes in silence—a man who is willing to wait forever for you to begin. My parents stayed in the waiting room until it was their turn, waiting to see if I'd come out all right. Caught at that moment between past and future. Worried about their daughter who has been taking Quaaludes for fun, out with her friends on a beach in Santa Monica, unsupervised, her face unnaturally lit by bonfires. Behind those doors: I'm glowering in a chair, the room dim and cluttered. Ratty couch, scarred oak desk, swivel chair with a rip in the Naugahyde. Not a fancy doctor; we couldn't afford fancy. I refused to speak, or I made up stories that could pass as true, that could be plausible explanations. My parents were so quiet on the car ride there, my father's large hands gripping the steering wheel, radio tuned to a baseball game.

But now it's just me and my mother and Paul Harvey. His voice always soft, a little tinged with static, so it feels intimate—as if he really is telling you and only you the rest of the story through a secret back channel. Paul Harvey always seemed to be a car-radio voice, not a home-radio voice—something that belonged in transit, within the in-between spaces, neither here nor there, as stories often are.

I suspected, sometimes, that my mother took the long way home in order to hear *The Rest of the Story*, listening intently to the obscure historical tidbits, the odd current events, and Paul Harvey revealing the unknown that looms behind the already known. We could picture him in the studio behind a cluttered desk, speaking into his big microphone, the chuckle in his voice as he divulged the big surprise.

In later years, I'll hear Paul Harvey again, as a more grown-up girl behind the wheel of my own car, a fragment of my face reflected in the rearview mirror. Or I'll be a passenger next to a boyfriend, my bare feet up on the dash, toes tilted toward the window as we move quickly through landscapes both familiar and strange. Paul Harvey's voice will provide a soothing balm, the rest of the story unfurling as the world flies by, obviating any need to speak.

I'll still be splitting hairs. I'll still find myself in therapists' offices, trying to explain something that can't be explained, to create a story out of ragged bits and pieces. Stories, I'll discover, don't always have neat resolutions or clever finales. Most often, they never end.

Paul Harvey concludes each segment with his tagline: *Well, folks, that's the rest of the story!* and the music swells, then a commercial—Paul Harvey hawking soap or cigarettes or cars—and my mother clicks the radio off. We drive the rest of the way home in the quiet car, wheels humming their transient tune, my mother smoking down the last of her cigarette. She stubs it out while every mirror flashes the light of the setting sun.

Surface Tension

I

1968: On summer mornings, my father skims the surface of our Doughboy swimming pool. The long-handled net slides gracefully, picking up all that doesn't belong: walnut leaves, dead beetles, the wings of dragonflies. He reaches long, slides the net in a full arc, dumps the contents over the side, and does it again. I watch him from my bedroom window.

I watch him sweep the pool with an elegance previously invisible in any of the males I know; I have two brothers who are clumsy with their affections, who hardly see me as they careen down the hallways or slam the screen door. And my father has knobby elbows and knees, usually hurrying to get something done. In his wedding picture, he looks to be all ears and chin, with a wide, v-shaped grin.

The white net captures any stray litter floating atop the antiseptic blue water. For debris below the surface—a Band-Aid, a barrette, a coin—he'll have to don his bathing trunks and jump in, wading with long strides to where the offending item gleams. Or he'll get one of us to do it and make it a game. I'll dive in headfirst, my legs scissoring out behind me, chlorine burning my nose. I'll scramble with my eyes shut to pick the bottom clean.

My father smiles as he sweeps the pool, and it is, I can tell, a kind of contemplation for him; it's work that he can do quietly, by himself, and the rewards of his labor become immediately clear. He can do this job well, returning things to where they belong, to *how* they belong.

My mother might be watching too, from the screen door in the living room, as she stands with a can of Pledge in hand. She takes pleasure in a shiny end table, a spotless sink. She has told me several times, *A man likes a clean sink*, while scrubbing with the Brillo pad and rinsing till everything shines.

II

2010: Last fall, my parents visited me in my newly remodeled home. I gave them my bedroom, as I always do, and slept upstairs on the futon below the eaves, with my dog and cat for company. I had scrubbed every corner of the house, wanted us all to make a good impression.

One morning, I glanced in my bedroom and saw my father sitting on the edge of my bed, his back to me, arms draped on his knees, simply looking out the front windows. Perhaps he was only resting a minute before standing up, but I saw something in the posture of his back: some resignation, perhaps, in the curve of his spine, or a patient melancholy in his gaze. It was only a second, but his posture made me look again, then I continued back upstairs.

When I first moved into this house ten years ago, my father built me two window boxes to go under those bedroom windows. They held up only a year before I had to hire a professional to rebuild them. He and my mom helped me paint the kitchen, a messy project, and we did a terrible job; I had to repaint when I added on the dining room. He mentions both these things all the time, ruefully shaking his head.

When I was in graduate school, he built me a reading stand: a knock-off version of the expensive props you could buy in the Levenger catalog; it held your book or papers at an angle to save your neck and your eyes. It was serviceable, not elegant, and I did use it for several years, pulling it out and balancing it on my lap. Then it became too bulky, too rough, and I let it languish in a closet. Recently, in a fit of cleaning, I pulled it out and placed it on the curb, along with a pile of other old items, with a "Free" sign perched on top. One by one, all the other things disappeared, except for that reading stand, until it sat forlornly on the edge of the street alone. I took it back inside, couldn't bear to throw it away.

My father wants nothing more than to make useful things, to be a useful person. He has systems for everything. On this visit, he was happiest when helping me hang wind chimes on my deck; he teetered on the footstool, ignoring my mother's pleas to get down, to allow me to grab the ladder from my neighbor's shed. He wanted to do it all himself, to hang these chimes with his own hands, without us women harping at him. He screwed in the hook with quick sharp twists, and hung the chimes perfectly. A simple job, but still done right.

My parents bought me these chimes as a housewarming present. When we walked into the garden store, dozens of chimes swayed overhead: some sounding out bass notes like gongs, others twinkling in high registers that sounded like birds. It was difficult to choose, but I kept coming back to these—a set tuned to a pentatonic scale that let forth the simplest music in the world.

I once visited St. Olaf College in Minnesota where, in the center of campus, they've built a gazebo graced with many chimes to commemorate students who died while enrolled at the school. Each chime is tuned to the key of D major, the key of many hymns, and someone has engraved each one with a student's name. "On windy days," the college brochure describes, "the sound of the chimes can be heard almost everywhere on campus." I sat in that gazebo, closed my eyes, and felt myself surrounded by the voices of the dead.

In the seventeenth and eighteenth centuries, musicians ascribed to each key its own particular emotional color. In a German treatise written in 1806, the key of D major is described as "the key of triumph, of Hallelujahs, of war-cries, of victory-rejoicing." By contrast, the key of D# minor incites "feelings of the anxiety of the soul's deepest distress, of brooding despair, of blackest depression, of the most gloomy condition of the soul. . . . If ghosts could speak, their speech would approximate this key."

The ghosts at St. Olaf seem full of rejoicing. But it's such a short distance from Hallelujah to Despair. One wrong note could do you in.

III

My parents and I get lost as I take them to the cruise terminal in Vancouver, B.C.—there's some kind of festival going on downtown that clogs the already busy one-way streets—so by the time we get there I'm tired and stressed, and the hoped-for farewell picnic we were going to have is not going to happen. The parking attendants wave us into a loading zone, and I pull the heavy luggage out of the car. A porter immediately whisks the bags away to the *Coral Princess*, an enormous ship waiting dockside to take my parents to Alaska.

Okay, now I'm nervous, my mother says, glancing at the boat, biting back tears. *It will be fun*, I say, *so much fun*, in the same bright, encouraging voice she used on me the first day of junior high. It didn't work then, and it doesn't work now. But it's a voice both of us seem to use more and more these days: helpful, wheedling, full of forced cheer.

The attendants want me to move my car, so I give my parents a quick hug goodbye, and I know they must be hungry—we didn't have our lunch. I turn back to watch them: my mother so thin, with the look on her face she gets when she's nervous, the eyes scrunched up, watching my father, who himself is hunched over and looks frail. I want to call them back, say, *Here's your lunch* and *zip up your coat.* I want to write their names and address on the inner linings of their jackets with a Sharpie in case they get lost. But there are cars circling, jockeying for a loading spot, so I get in my car, roll up the windows, and drive away.

But I keep seeing them there, about to pass through a gateway to a ship that will take them somewhere they've never been, a place they're still not sure they want to go. I keep remembering that brief glimpse I had of my father, sitting with his back to me on my bed, something so heavy in his shoulders, his hands still in his lap. He could have just been pausing as he put on his shoes, or admiring the pansies in the window box, thinking of nothing at all. Still I could have said something, something encouraging, but I didn't; I kept on going, and now they're gone, the ghost of my father still heavy on my bed, yearning for something I don't know how to give.

When I get home, I hear the chimes on the back deck. I hear them the minute I step foot in the house, a melody both startling and sweet.

IV

2011: The next time I visit my parents my mom is in the hospital. She had an "episode," as my father put it: her blood pressure dropped to a dangerous level, and she got dizzy, nearly blacked out. The paramedics, when they did the emergency EKG, found an irregular heartbeat and whisked her off to the hospital, my father following behind.

This all happened the day before I'd planned to visit their home in Arizona. I was out doing last-minute errands, and when I got home I had several messages from my father telling me to cancel the whole trip. We now wouldn't be able to do what we'd planned: drive together to California to see my little brother and his family, to celebrate Hanukkah in their new house. *But I still want to see you*, I said. *I can still come to see you.* They hadn't seemed to consider that an option.

When I arrive, my father greets me at the airport, still wearing his "Visitor" sticker from the hospital. It's odd to see him alone there; in the dozens of times I've visited my parents, it's always the two of them at the gate, both of them waving and waving. *She's okay*, he says. *It's okay.*

And she is. Once she got some fluids in her she stabilized, but because she's had a history of heart problems they're keeping her in for tests, lots of tests. Without her makeup her face looks pale, tired, and her hair sticks up on the back of her head. But she's smiling, and kind, as always, to all the people ministering about her.

The second day I offer to give her a little massage, and when I pull up my seat next to her, she giggles, turns to me, our faces closer than they've been since I was a baby. *I love you*, she laughs, then she lies back and closes her eyes. I don't really know how to negotiate around the hospital bed, but I do the best I can. My father gets something stuck in his throat and he begins coughing, has to step outside. My mother murmurs, *Go check on your father*, but I don't; I keep my hands on her shoulder, then her shins, then her feet.

As I massage my mother, my hands grow lighter and lighter, until it feels as though I'm hovering over a membrane of water. Water has surface tension—its molecules bond so tightly together that even heavy things, if distributed evenly enough, will stay afloat. I'm touching her without really touching her. Her face relaxes. On her shins I feel currents skittering up and down; on her feet my hands become warm as hot stones. When I finish, I brush the air above her body, just as a nurse's aid comes in to take more blood.

V

When my father and I return to their house, I can see he's really lost without his wife. They've been married fifty-eight years, and each one has their defined roles; it's too much for him to do by himself. The vacuums are out where their vacuuming was interrupted. The dog's water bowl is empty. He has a list for everything: bring in mail, deal with the head of lettuce. The bed is unmade. He counts out his pills, then loses them.

I offer to help him with the household receipts. This is something my mother and father do together; the task is overdue, and so I sit next to him at his desk and read off the dates and amounts on the receipts while he enters them into Quicken. I pick up each one, search for the date, tell him where the purchase was made, read off the amount: $4.38, $22.95, $12.77. They did a lot of shopping on 11/29. They bought a lot of small things. The receipts make up a little narrative of their day—the errands, then a matinee, then an early dinner for $5.50 at the burrito place near the theater. That would have been a good day, and they would have been home in time to feed the dogs, a task that seems to take them a long time, since each dog requires her own particular ministrations.

We're in the bedroom; his desk takes up one corner by the sliding glass door. Behind us their bed sits disheveled, and the poodle sleeps on top of my mother's pillow, her eyes at half-mast. The older dog is in her bed, asleep; it's difficult for her to get up these days, and she's hard of hearing, though when we arrived she seemed wiggly as a puppy, so happy to see us; she must have been convinced she'd never see any of us again. Both of them keep looking for my mother, bewildered at her absence.

I stop commenting on the receipts; I get into the rhythm of this task, reading off the numbers while my father types them in, the computer sorting them automatically into neat categories. I ask him if he would teach me how to do it; my own finances are a mess, and I always have just a vague idea of where my money goes. This request perks him up. *Of course*, he says, *it's easy when you get the hang of it*, and we continue the work together, making manageable all these bits and pieces of a life, sweeping them clean.

To Live For

I'd like to imagine that, when he comes to my door, I'd invite Death in for a cup of tea, some sliced apples with cinnamon and slivered almonds—a healthy snack—and we'd chat about the unseasonable weather. Then he'd stand up, stretch, say: *Okay, I guess it's time to be going,* and carry our dishes to the sink like any good guest. I'd pat my dog where she sleeps in her bed with one eye open—she'd licked Death's hand, rolled over for him as she does for any visitor—and I'd slick the cat's forehead with my thumb, walk out the back door, into the yard with the lawn mown by an unseen hand. We'd just keep walking toward the apple tree with its wizened Gravensteins.

The dog would be on the back deck now, quizzical, one ear up and one ear down, muzzle sniffing the air—that would bring me to my senses, pull me up short. I'd say: *Oh, I'm sorry, there's been a mistake, I can't go with you now, the dog, you know.* . . . And I'd nod in her direction. Death would look back, loosen his grip on my elbow, say: *Well, a dog's not enough to keep you here, really; I mean we'd have to get a special dispensation. Think of all the young mothers with kids—everyone has something they have to leave behind, I mean, that's kind of the* point *of the whole thing* . . .

And as he goes on and on about the finer aspects of death—about how death really *requires* such a leave-taking, about how death makes you see how *transient,* how *illusive,* all these attachments really are—I'd just slip away, quietly sidle up the lawn until I sat on the top step with my dog, her nose in my ear, then sniffing all along my neck, snorting her satisfaction at my return, eager to know where I have been and why.

I remember a conversation I had with my neighbor once, a single woman like me, her mother going through painful chemotherapy to give her a few more months to live. We asked each other: *Would you do it, would you stay alive at all costs?* And we both kind of smiled, a little embarrassed, said, *No, I don't have that much to live for. . . .* And it sounded not morbid, no hint of self-pity, just a statement of fact, something that actually felt quite liberating, *not much to live for*—no husbands, no kids, a few friends who might miss us, but the feeling would pass—so that when the time came we could perhaps take that stroll with no reason to look back.

But now, while Death keeps talking to himself under the apple tree, gesturing this way and that with his scythe (a curved blade I can see now is rather rusty, rather dull), I have a small dog curling into my side, a dog whose fur feels like silk, whose rhythmic breathing synchronizes with my pulse, and this small body would be enough—more than enough—to keep me here even just a few seconds longer.

This dog might decide to run out into her yard and welcome Death back, because to her everyone is a friend, and I won't call her off, not yet, because there's something golden in her that will keep her unharmed—she can run toward Death and I can watch her, I can sit on my back porch and feel only the weight of her on my lap in the evening, in my little house, while my great-grandmothers gaze down from their framed portraits on the mantel.

I imagine each of them knows that nothing's ever left behind. We become what we become: a sifting of particles in the air, and

Brenda Miller

I wonder who of us will go next with this chatty stranger into the orchard—the apples smelling of cider, the pears buzzing with wasps, and cherries vanishing into the gullets of starlings and crows.

EPILOGUE

We Regret to Inform You

April 12, 1970

Dear Young Artist:

Thank you for your attempt to draw a tree. We appreciate your efforts, especially the way you sat patiently on the sidewalk, gazing at that tree for an hour before setting pen to paper, and the many quick strokes of charcoal you executed with enthusiasm. But your smudges look nothing like a tree. In fact, they look like nothing at all, and the pleasure and pride you take in the work are not enough to redeem it. We are pleased to offer you remedial training in the arts, but we cannot accept your "drawing" for display.

With regret and best wishes,
The Art Class
Andasol Avenue Elementary School

Brenda Miller

February 12, 1973

Dear Ninth-Grade Girl:

We regret to inform you that no suitable match has been found to
accompany you to the school dance. The volume of requests we
receive makes individual feedback impossible, but please know
that you were given careful consideration. Do feel free to attend on
your own, perhaps with another rejectee, and stand awkwardly in
a corner with a glass of warm punch in your sweaty hand. Watching others have a good time is excellent preparation for the roles
you will play in the future.

Best,
The Boys' Council of Patrick Henry Junior High

October 13, 1974

Dear Tenth-Grader:

Thank you for your application to be the girlfriend of one of our star basketball players. As you can imagine, we have received hundreds of similar requests and so cannot possibly respond personally to every one. This letter is to inform you that you have not been chosen for one of the coveted positions, but we do invite you to continue hanging around the lockers, acting as if you belong there. This selfless act will help the team members learn the art of ignoring lovesick girls.

Sincerely,
The Granada Hills Highlanders

P.S. Though your brother is one of the star players, we could not take this familial relationship into account. Sorry to say no! Please do try out for one of the rebound-girlfriend positions in the future.

Brenda Miller

November 15, 1975

Dear Prospective Dancer:

Thank you for trying out to be a Highland Dancer. Although we
know you looked forward to wearing the cute kilt and argyle knee
socks, the crisp white dress shirt and the tasseled shoes, we regret
to inform you that you did not make the cut into the second round
of auditions. Some girls simply are not coordinated enough to be
a member of this elite troupe. It's not your fault; you just haven't
quite "grown into" your body yet. We wish you the best of luck in
finding your niche elsewhere.

The Highland Dance Team
Granada Hills High School

January 15, 1977

Dear Future Thespian:

Thank you for choosing drama as your major at Cal State Northridge. While we are not the most prestigious acting school in the Greater Los Angeles Area, we do take pride in having a rigorous curriculum that requires all students to be fluent in diction, singing, movement arts, and a certain indefinable "something," a *je ne sais quoi* that gives a young woman presence on the stage.

Unfortunately you do not have what it takes to be a star and will always be relegated to the "second girl" or the waitress with one or two lines that you'll belt out with imperfect timing. We understand that in high school you got to play Emily in *Our Town,* watching the townsfolk from your perch in the afterlife, and that once you had a leading role in *The Effect of Gamma Rays on Man-in-the-Moon Marigolds,* but you delivered your lines too earnestly and were too eager to please.

We appreciate that you love turning into someone else for the space of an hour or so, and that you feel exhilarated once you hit your mark. But your lisping voice and rather clumsy gestures force us to look elsewhere for a leading lady. You might have more luck in a behind-the-scenes role—perhaps writing? It's come to our attention that you once wrote a one-act play called *Backstage,* which consisted of two stagehands waiting for the stage manager to arrive; the manager never arrives, and even the play itself is an illusion! Cute.

With best wishes,
The Cal State Northridge Drama Department

Brenda Miller

December 10, 1978

Dear College Dropout:

Thank you for the short time you spent with us. We understand
that you have decided to terminate your stay, a decision that seems
completely reasonable, given the circumstances. After all, who
knew that the semester you decided to come to UC Berkeley would
be so tumultuous. That unsavory business with Jim Jones and his
Bay Area followers left us all reeling. And then Harvey Milk was
shot, a blast that reverberated across the Bay. It truly did feel as
if the world were falling apart—we know that. We understand
why you took refuge in the music of the Grateful Dead, dancing
until you felt yourself leave your body, caught up in their brand
of enlightenment.

And given that you were a drama major, struggling on a campus
well known for histrionics and unrest—well, it's only understand-
able that you'd need some time to "find yourself." You're really too
young to be in such a big city on your own. When you had your exit
interview with the Dean of Students, you were completely inar-
ticulate about your reasons for leaving, perhaps because you still
have no idea what they are. You know there is a boy you might love
in Santa Cruz. You fed him peanuts at a Dead show. You imagine
playing house with him, living there in the shadows of tall trees.

But of course you couldn't say that to the Dean, as he swiveled in
his chair, looking so official in his gray suit. He clasped his hands
on the oak desk and waited for you to explain yourself. His office
looked out on the quad, where you'd heard the Talking Heads play
just a week earlier, and beyond that the dorm where the gentleman

you know only as "Pink Cloud" provided you with LSD, which you took in order to experience more fully the secrets the Dead whispered in your ear. You told the Dean none of this, but simply shrugged your shoulders and began to cry, at which point the Dean cleared his throat and wished you luck.

We regret to inform you that it will be quite a while before you grow up, and it will take some cataclysmic events in your life before you really begin to find the role that suits you. In any case, we wish you the best in all your future educational endeavors.

Sincerely,
UC Berkeley Registrar

October 26, 1979

Dear Potential Mom,

Thank you for providing a host home for each of us during the few weeks we stayed in residence. It was lovely but, in the end, didn't quite work out. Though we tried to be unobtrusive in our exit, the narrowness of your fallopian tubes made some damage unavoidable. Sorry about that. You know you were too young to have children anyway, right? And you know it wasn't your fault, not really. (Though you could have been a *tad* more careful in your carnal acts. But, no matter. Water under the bridge.)

We enjoyed our brief stay in your body and wish you the best of luck in conceiving children in the future.

With gratitude,
Ira and Isabelle

November 3, 1979

Dear Patient:

We regret to inform you that due to reproductive abnormalities, you will not be able to conceive children. *Barren* is not a word we use these days, but you may use it if you so choose. Your two miscarriages were merely symptoms of these abnormalities, which we surmise were acquired in utero. It's not your fault, but you may choose to take this misfortune as a sign of God's displeasure and torture yourself with guilt and self-loathing for many years to come.

All the best,
Student Health Center
Humboldt State University

Brenda Miller

June 2, 1982

Dear Little Raven:

Thank you for your three-year audition to serve as the white girl-friend and savior to a Native American man twelve years your senior. Your persistence has been admirable, but we regret to inform you that we can no longer use your services.

Yes, we appreciate the fact that you smoked tobacco in a cherry-wood pipe and wore a turquoise eagle around your neck. You listened to drums and chanting for hours on end and read *Black Elk Speaks* and got yourself an "Indian name." These efforts have all been noted. But the role of "pseudo-Native American white girl" is not one we can recommend.

We appreciate the many times you took this man to the hospital or let him borrow your car, your money, your time. But we're sure that if you take a good hard look at your performance, you'll see that you were using this relationship as punishment for your past sins. That kind of arrangement is never good for anyone. So we bid you farewell and wish you the best of luck as you seek spiritual salvation elsewhere.

Sincerely,
Yurok Elders

May 23, 1986

Dear Gatekeeper:

Thank you for your four years of service with Orr Hot Springs Resort, and in particular your role as live-in girlfriend to one of our older shareholders. We also appreciate your services as both a godmother to our resident toddler and confidante to his parents.

So it is with great sadness that we must inform you that your services are no longer required. This dismissal in no way reflects upon your job performance. (Well, you could have cleaned the lodge a little better and been a little more thorough when it was your turn to scrub the bathhouse.) It's simply time for you to move on.

Please pack your meager belongings into the car you bought for $200. Please do not dramatically extend the farewells, wandering the property to "say goodbye" to inanimate objects, to the gardens, to Tub Room #2, where you spent so many mornings immersed in yourself. Please do not throw the *I-Ching* to determine your next steps or read the tarot or take Ecstasy. Simply get into your car and chug up the mountain road at first light. You will feel a sensation of tearing—like a ligament ripped from the bone—but don't worry. This is normal. You will head north. You will be fine. You will find the role that suits you.

Namasté,
Orr Hot Springs Resort
Ukiah, California

Brenda Miller

April 14, 1994

Dear Potential Wife:

Thank you for your application to be my spouse. While I see much to admire here, I regret to inform you that you do not meet my needs at this time.

I do want to commend you for your efforts over the past five years. You did your best, but your anxiety made it difficult to proceed. Even so, we did love our coffee in the morning, our home-cooked meals in the evening, our travels through the Middle East. (Let's just forget the argument we had while walking the walls of the Old City in Jerusalem. Water under the bridge.) You laughed at my jokes; thanks for that. And of course it was fun being fledgling writers together, before reality intervened.

Try to remember that we loved the only way we could: not perfectly, nor entirely well, but genuinely. I adored your lisp and the little mole above your lip. I touched your scars, and you touched mine. We tried. But at some point in a relationship you shouldn't have to try so hard, right?

It may just be bad timing. Best wishes in your future matrimonial endeavors. I'm sure your talents will be put to good use elsewhere. I hope we can remain friends.

Your Grad-School Boyfriend

June 30, 1999

Dear Applicant:

Thank you for your query about assuming the role of stepmother to two young girls. While we found your résumé impressive, we regret to inform you that we have decided not to fill the position this year. You did ask for feedback on your application, so we have the following to suggest:

1. You do not yet understand the delicate emotional dynamic that rules a divorced father's relationship with his children. The children will always, *always*, come first, trumping any needs you may have. You will understand this in a few years, but for now you still require some apprenticeship training.

2. Though you have sacrificed your time and energy to support this family, it's become clear that your desire to be a step-mother stems from some deep-seated wound in yourself, a wound you are trying to heal using these children. They have enough to deal with—an absent mother, a frazzled father—they don't need your traumas entering the mix.

3. Seeing the movie *Stepmom* is not an actual tutorial on step-parenting.

4. On Mother's Day you should not expect flowers, gifts, or even a thank-you. You are not their mother.

5. You are still a little delusional about the potential here for a long-term relationship. The father is not ready to commit so

soon after a messy divorce. (This should have been obvious to you when he refused to hold your hand, citing that it made him feel "claustrophobic." Can you not take a hint?)

We hope this feedback is helpful, and we wish you the best in your future parenting endeavors.

xxx ooo
Your ex-boyfriend's family

January 3, 2007

Dear New Dog Owner:

Congratulations on adopting your first dog! She will surely provide hours of love and enjoyment and be a wonderful addition to your family.

Here are a few tips:

1. A dog is not a child, even if you do call yourself "Mom." Yes, other people will now know you as "Abbe's Mom," and you'll take a great deal of foolish pride in this. But, remember, a dog is not a child.

2. Though a dog is not a child, you will need to plan your life around this creature: food, water, companionship, play dates, illnesses. Yes, there will be illnesses. You will need to make crucial decisions while in tears at the vet's office. You may need to empty your savings account to insure that your dog is no longer in pain.

3. You will at some point say to yourself: *I don't need to date; I have my dog.* Be very careful about repeating this statement in public.

4. You will grow fond of this dog and overlook her shortcomings, her flaws. (Really, they are so few.) Why can't you do this with a man?

5. A pet's love, contrary to popular belief, is not unconditional.

There are many conditions: expensive food, regular walks, toys, your undivided attention.

6. A dog such as Abbe makes a terrific all-natural antidepressant. At some level, of course, you already know this; otherwise you wouldn't have spent so much more time on Petfinder.com rather than on Match.com. When you are with her, you will feel as if something were being repaired in your body, like a ligament rejoining to bone.

7. At times you'll feel rejected by Abbe. Don't worry, this is normal. Though she is very friendly, Abbe needs her space sometimes. (As do we all!)

8. You will train to be a therapy-dog team, providing companionship and affection to people in hospitals and nursing homes. Though Abbe will be better at it than you are, you'll enjoy sitting by her side as she is petted by strangers young and old. You'll stay quiet and simply observe, playing a background role, finding satisfaction in this. You'll understand that such therapy is as much for you as it is for them.

Once again, congratulations on taking on this huge responsibility. It's an indication of maturity, of finding your niche and settling into your life as it is.

Best wishes,
Furbaby Pet Rescue of Whatcom County

Acknowledgments

Many of these essays first appeared, sometimes in slightly different form, in *Arts & Letters, Brevity, Creative Nonfiction, Fourth Genre, Fugue, Los Angeles Review, New Ohio Review, Ninth Letter, Passages North, River Teeth, Seneca Review, The Sun, Triquarterly,* and *Water~Stone Review.*

My prose e-chapbook, *Who You Will Become* (Shebooks Press, 2015), contains several of the short pieces in this collection.

With appreciation for my many writing angels. Here are a few: Lee Gulyas, Julie Marie Wade, Nancy Canyon, Katie Humes, Victoria Savage, Holly J. Hughes, Suzanne Paola, Bruce Beasley, Joel Long, and Tiana Kahakauwila.

Thank you to the stellar folks at Ovenbird Books, especially Stan Rubin and Kate Carroll de Gutes, and to Heather Weber for her fine copy editing. Also, my gratitude to Ellie A. Rogers for her excellent eye, and to Janet Fagan, for permission to use "Ghost Deer" as the emblem for this book.

Also, applause to the Helen Riaboff Whiteley Center, where much of this book was written.

And, always, my deep and abiding gratitude to Judith Kitchen.

Notes

The epigraph for "Beloved" is excerpted from the poem "Late Fragment," by Raymond Carver, in *A New Path to the Waterfall* (Atlantic Monthly Press, 1989).

The epigraph for "Gizzards" is excerpted from the poem "Another Empty Window Dipped in Milk," by Kelli Russell Agodon, in *Letters From the Emily Dickinson Room* (White Pine Press, 2010).

The epigraph for "36 Holes" is excerpted from the poem "River" by Catherine Barnett, in *Into Perfect Spheres Such Holes Are Pierced* (Alice James Books, 2004).

BRENDA MILLER is the author of four previous essay collections: *Who You Will Become, Listening Against the Stone, Blessing of the Animals,* and *Season of the Body*. She also co-authored *Tell It Slant: Creating, Refining, and Publishing Creative Nonfiction* and *The Pen and The Bell: Mindful Writing in a Busy World*. Her work has received six Pushcart Prizes. She is a Professor of English at Western Washington University, and serves as associate faculty at the Rainier Writing Workshop. She lives in Bellingham, WA, with her dog Abbe and a rotating crew of foster dogs who take up temporary residence.

ABOUT THE COVER ARTIST: Janet Fagan is an artist working in the Pacific Northwest. Inspired by the hours she spends moving through the landscape, "Ghost Deer" is one in a series of paintings and woodblock prints honoring the trails, open-spaces, and park-lands where Janet feels most at home. To see more of Janet's work please visit janetfagan.com.

OVENBIRD

JUDITH KITCHEN'S OVENBIRD BOOKS
The Circus Train by Judith Kitchen
An Earlier Life by Brenda Miller

JUDITH KITCHEN SELECT
Objects in Mirror Are Closer Than They Appear by Kate Carroll de Gutes
The Book of Knowledge and Wonder by Steven Harvey
The Last Good Obsession by Sandra Swinburne
Dear Boy: An Epistolary Memoir by Heather Weber
The Slow Farm by Tarn Wilson

WWW.OVENBIRDBOOKS.COM

CPSIA information can be obtained
at www.ICGtesting.com
Printed in the USA
FSOW01n2107201017
40178FS